Rencontres Culturelles

Cross-cultural mini-dramas

Arley W. Levno

Towson State University,
Baltimore, Maryland

Barbara Snyder
Consulting Editor

National Textbook Company
NTC a division of *NTC Publishing Group* • Lincolnwood, Illinois USA

1992 Printing

Published by National Textbook Company, a division of NTC Publishing Group.
© 1984, 1977 by NTC Publishing Group, 4255 West Touhy Avenue,
Lincolnwood (Chicago), Illinois 60646-1975 USA.
Manufactured in the United States of America.
Library of Congress Catalog Number: 77-78271

2 3 4 5 6 7 8 9 0 ML 9 8 7 6 5 4

How To Use This Book

The mini-dramas in this book involve American and French-speaking young people and their families. Most of the mini-dramas take place in France or in other French-speaking countries; some take place in the United States. Each mini-drama involves an encounter between a French-speaking person and an American, and illustrates a cultural conflict. Each drama is followed by a question relating to differences in culture. Four choices are provided as possible answers to the question. The student should choose what he or she considers to be the correct answer and then turn to the indicated follow-up explanation to check the answer. The follow-up will explain why the answer is correct, or, if it is wrong, it will explain why the answer is not correct.

The mini-dramas help bring about understanding of cultural differences. When people travel in French-speaking countries, knowing about some of these differences help them understand people from different cultures and, therefore, bring about better cross-cultural understanding.

Contents

Introduction

In a world brought ever closer by jet travel and modern telecommunications, *Rencontres culturelles* fills a distinct and important need. Increasingly, men and women from different cultures are coming in contact and having to learn the sometimes difficult lesson of how to communicate with one another. These encounters with people from different countries and cultures can be full of surprises and cause unforeseen problems. This book deals directly with such cultural dilemmas. Each mini-drama in this volume illustrates the fact that values, attitudes, life-styles, expectations, beliefs, and roles tend to be conceived in a different way in a different country.

At the end of each mini-drama, students are asked a question and given four possible solutions. They are then directed to check their answers. If they choose an incorrect answer the first time, they are given clues and further information to help them find the right solution.

The mini-dramas may serve equally well as supplementary material, as a self-study text, or as a mini-course. Units are arranged according to language difficulty. However, they are self-contained. Thus, the various concepts treated may be discussed in the order in which they arise in the basal text you are using. Since there are 50 mini-dramas in *Rencontres culturelles,* they may be used at a rate of about one a week during a single year, or two a month over two years.

Three basic objectives guided the author in preparing this cultural material: (1) Students will appreciate that cultural differences, not just language differences, exist between and among countries; (2) Students traveling to a French-speaking country will experience fewer difficulties due to cultural conflict; and (3) If a culture conflict does occur, a student will be able to resolve it intelligently because of the experience he or she has had in testing hypotheses. In this way, the traumas of "culture shock" will be significantly reduced.

In connection with these cultural mini-dramas, the teacher may lead students in a discussion that brings out the relativity of cultural expressions. Such a discussion could make the point that there is not one right way of thinking or acting—that there may be a variety of legitimate responses. For additional work, students might continue the dialogue at the point where the American begins to understand. They might also write a new mini-drama that shows the American student responding appropriately to the situation.

The author hopes that *Rencontres culturelles* will encourage students to deepen their knowledge of foreign cultures and foreign languages and that it will promote increased understanding of cultural diversity. Other National Textbook Company publications also contribute to these objectives. *Teaching Culture: Strategies for Foreign Language Educators* by H. Ned Seelye discusses the development of cultural skills and describes the process by which we acquire cultural traits. *Encuentros culturales* in Spanish, *Incontri culturali* in Italian, and *Kulturelle Begegnungen* in German present cross-cultural mini-dramas patterned like those in this book. *The Magazine* and *The Newspaper* are sets of spirit duplicating masters that provide practice in evaluating cultural elements through the study of excerpts taken from actual French publications.

1. Invité chez les Français

Family life

Diane, assistante d'anglais dans un lycée,° parle ici avec l'assistant d'allemand, Franz. Rouen, France.

Franz: Nous sommes dans ce lycée depuis° six mois, et je commence à mieux° comprendre les Français.

Diane: Oui, moi aussi. Mais quand même,° il y a une chose que je n'arrive pas à comprendre au sujet des Français.

Franz: Qu'est-ce que c'est?

Diane: C'est que les Français n'invitent pas les étrangers chez eux. On t'a invité, toi?°

Franz: Oui, mais une seule fois.

Why haven't the French invited Diane and Franz to their homes more often?

A. The French, in general, are intimidated by teachers. (Turn to p. 53, A)

B. The French do not particularly like Americans and Germans. (Turn to p. 55, B)

C. The French rarely invite anyone except relatives to their homes. (Turn to p. 60, C)

D. The French invite guests into their homes only after they have known them for about a year. (Turn to p. 66, D)

---

lycée secondary school   **depuis** since   **mieux** better
quand même even so   **On t'a invité, toi?** Have they invited you?

2. Jean-Marie Devreux

Language, religion

Jerry et Pierre partagent° une chambre dans une résidence universitaire à l'Université de Montréal. L'Université de Montréal, Canada.

Jerry: Pierre, il y a une lettre pour toi.
Pierre: C'est une lettre de mes parents, sans doute.
Jerry: Non, c'est une lettre d'une jeune fille.
Pierre: Ah, oui?
Jerry: Ah, voilà la lettre de cette jeune fille. Oui, elle s'appelle Jean-Marie Devreux.
Pierre: (Il rit.°) Mais, c'est impossible, Jerry.
Jerry: Pourquoi ris-tu, Pierre?

Why did Pierre laugh?

A.   Pierre was happy. He did not expect a letter from that particular girl. (Turn to p. 95, A)
B.   Jean-Marie is a boy's name. (Turn to p. 93, B)
C.   The letter is actually from two people, Jean and Marie Devreux. (Turn to p. 94, C)
D.   Jerry badly mispronounced the name Jean-Marie Devreux. (Turn to p. 92, D)

---

partagent share   **Il rit** He laughs

3. Des Rencontres

Social proprieties, language, youth culture

Au restaurant universitaire du Centre Bullier à Paris.

John: Bonjour les Françaises. Je m'appelle John Frederick, et voici mon camarade, Paul Schmidt. Comment vous appelez-vous?

Jacqueline: Voilà Marie-Noële Dupont et moi, je m'appelle Jacqueline Martin.

Paul: Enchanté, Marie-Noële et Jacqueline. Jacqueline, veux-tu me passer du pain, s'il te plaît. . . .Merci. Quels cours suis-tu° à l'université, Marie-Noële?

Marie-Noële: La chimie. . . . Bon! Jacqueline, on s'en va?° (Les deux jeunes filles partent.)

John: They sure didn't want to talk with us.

Paul: No. They're not very friendly. I guess French girls are just that way.

Why did the French girls leave?

A. French girls do not like American men. (Turn to p. 56, A)
B. Thc girls do not want to get involved with strangers. (Turn to p. 61, R)
C. French women are rather cold. (Turn to p. 53, C)
D. The girls had to rush off to class. (Turn to p. 60, D)

Quels cours suis-tu What courses are you taking
on s'en va? shall we go?

4. Allons jouer au football

Language, leisure-time activities

Didier vient d'arriver aux Etats-Unis de la Martinique pour passer un mois chez une famille américaine. Denver, Colorado.

Peter: Didier, vous aimez les sports?

Didier: Oui, certains sports. J'aime le football.

Peter: Formidable! Moi aussi. Allons jouer un peu. Let's play some catch.

Didier: Parlez français, s'il vous plaît. Je ne comprends pas "play some catch".

Peter: Moi, je vais prendre le ballon dans les mains et je vais vous le lancer. °

Didier: Ah, je comprends. Vous parliez du basketball. Je comprends "play catch".

Peter: Non, je parlais° toujours du football.

Didier: Mais il ne faut pas toucher le ballon avec les mains quand on joue au football.

Peter: (A lui-même°) Didier ne sait pas jouer au football, c'est clair. °

Why does Didier say that one is not supposed to touch the ball with the hands?

A. What Didier is talking about is called *football* in France. (Turn to p. 92, A)

B. Didier does not know how to play football. (Turn to p. 95, B)

C. Didier was confusing basketball with football. (Turn to p. 93, C)

D. Didier does not understand English very well. (Turn to p. 94, D)

---

lancer to throw   **je parlais** I was talking
(A lui-même) To himself   **c'est clair** it's obvious

5. Tu as ton permis?

Education, family life, leisure-time activities

Henri, étudiant de l'Université de Nantes passe un mois aux Etats-Unis chez une famille américaine. La Nouvelle Orléans, Louisiane.

Chuck: Henri, tu as ton permis de conduire?°
Henri: Non, pas encore. Je n'ai pas beaucoup d'occasions de conduire° notre auto. Et toi, tu as ton permis?
Chuck: Oui, bien sûr. Autrement, je n'aurais pas le droit° de conduire mon auto. Quelle sorte de voiture ta famille a-t-elle?
Henri: Nous avons une Peugeot. C'est une belle voiture de très bonne qualité, selon mon père. C'est lui qui la conduit.
Chuck: Ah, oui?

Why does Henri not have a car?

A. University students in France generally do not earn enough money while working part-time during the school year and full-time during the summer to pay for a car. (Turn to p. 62, A)
B. French parents usually do not permit their children to buy cars while attending school. (Turn to p. 57, B)
C. The French standard of living is quite low compared to ours, so most families do not have cars. (Turn to p. 65, C)
D. Because of high government taxes on automobiles, an automobile costs about twice as much in France as in the United States. (Turn to p. 56, D)

---

permis de conduire driver's license
je n'aurais pas le droit I would not have the right

conduire to drive

6. Des Poètes-chanteurs

The arts, leisure-time activities

Sens, France.

James: Tu aimes la musique, Anne?

Anne: Oui, j'aime les chanteurs populaires, mais j'ai une petite préférence pour la musique classique.

James: Connais-tu° des chanteurs populaires américains?

Anne: Oui, quelques-uns.° Mais ils chantent presque toujours des chansons d'amour. On finit par s'ennuyer de° ces mêmes thèmes.

James: Les chansons folkloriques américaines ne sont pas toujours des chansons d'amour, tu sais.

Anne: Oui, mais il y a certains chanteurs français qui traitent des thèmes très différents. Je parle des chansons de Brassens, de Brel, de Ferré de Moustaki, de Ferrat, etc.

James: Ils chantent des chansons folkloriques, n'est-ce pas?

Anne: Non, ce n'est pas ça.

Why doesn't James understand what kind of songs Anne is talking about?

A. James, never having heard such songs, is trying to compare them with American folk songs. (Turn to p. 90, A)

B. James only likes sentimental love songs. (Turn to p. 91, B)

C. James has never heard French pop music. (Turn to p. 89, C)

D. James has never been to France before. (Turn to p. 88, D)

Connais-tu Do you know   **quelques-uns** some of them
On finit par s'ennuyer de One finally becomes bored with

7.   Le Service n'est pas compris!

Social proprieties, leisure-time activities

Au théâtre, Bruxelles, Belgique.

Vieille dame: Les billets,° s'il vous plaît, monsieur.
Harold: Oui, les voilà, madame.
    (Elle prend les billets et guide Harold et Mary à leurs places.)
Vieille dame: Voilà vos places, monsieur, madame.
Harold: Merci, madame.
    (Ils prennent leurs places.)
Vieille dame: (Elle les regarde sévèrement.) Monsieur! Le service n'est pas compris!
Harold: (A sa femme) I didn't understand that. What does she mean by "Le service n'est pas compris."?
Mary: I have no idea, but she's sure furious with us.

What did the woman want to communicate to the two Americans?

A. They had taken the wrong seats. (Turn to p. 70, A)
B. She does not like Americans. (Turn to p. 66, B)
C. They had not given her a tip. (Turn to p. 67, C)
D. She felt insulted because of a misunderstanding of what Harold said to her. (Turn to p. 62, D)

---

les billets the tickets

8. Le Débrouillard

Liberty, individualism

A la douane° française, à la frontière franco-espagnole. Hendaye, France.

Pierre: Ecoute, mon vieux,° peux-tu me rendre un petit service?
Jim: Comme tu veux. Qu'est-ce que c'est?
Pierre: C'est que, selon le règlement,° j'ai le droit d'apporter en France deux boîtes° de cigares de Havane. Eh bien, j'en ai quatre. Veux-tu porter deux de ces boîtes pour moi? Autrement, on va me les confisquer à la douane.
Jim: Eh bien, je ne sais pas. Je suis étranger, tu sais. On pourrait m'arrêter° si on voit que je fais cela pour toi.

Why is Pierre asking Jim to do this favor?

A. Pierre is probably a trafficker in drugs. (Turn to p. 57, A)
B. Pierre actually doesn't like Jim and is trying to get him into trouble. (Turn to p. 64, B)
C. The French have little respect for laws. (Turn to p. 62, C)
D. The French often try to break minor regulations to get what they want. (Turn to p. 65, D)

---

la douane customs
selon le règlement according to the regulations
On pourrait m'arrêter They could arrest me

mon vieux my old pal
boîtes boxes

9.   Ça ne se fait pas!

Social proprieties, individualism

Madeleine Maubray fait un voyage avec son cousin américain d'origine française, Robert Maubray. Dans un wagon du train en route vers Paris.

Robert: Il fait bien chaud dans ce train n'est-ce pas?
Madeleine: Oui, dehors° il fait plus frais.
Robert: Ce que je ne comprends pas, c'est que tous ces hommes-là ont chaud au point de suer à grosses gouttes,° mais ils ne quittent pas° leurs vestons.
Madeleine: Ça ne se fait pas,° mon vieux.

Why do the Frenchmen on the train keep their coats on even when it is hot?

A. They keep their coats on for reasons of health. (Turn to p. 65, A)
B. They want to show off their nice clothes. (Turn to p. 67, B)
C. It keeps their white shirts clean. (Turn to p. 64, C)
D. It is the custom to keep the sport coat on in public. (Turn to p. 57, D)

---

dehors outside
ils ne quittent pas they do not take off

suer à grosses gouttes sweat profusely
Ça ne se fait pas That's just not done

10.   Sympathiques,° mais. . .

Family life, leisure-time activities

Deux Françaises habitent chez des familles américaines pendant l'été à Los Angeles, Californie.

Marie: Comment trouves-tu ta famille américaine?

Jeanne: Ils sont tous très sympathiques. Comment trouves-tu ta famille?

Marie: Chez moi aussi, ils sont très sympathiques quand je les rencontre à la maison.

Jeanne: Qu'est-ce que tu veux dire?°

Marie: Tout le monde a son club, son équipe sportive, ses cours du soir. Ils sont rarement à la maison.

Jeanne: Ma famille est un peu comme ça aussi.

Marie: Je vois que les parents et les enfants se réunissent très peu. Ils n'ont pas le temps.

Jeanne: Oui, ils n'ont peut-être pas de sentiments profonds les uns pour les autres.

Why do Jeanne and Marie think the members of American families do not have strong sentiments for each other?

A.   The girls are jealous that they are not as active socially as Americans. (Turn to p. 93, A)

B.   The girls want more attention. (Turn to p. 94, B)

C.   In the U.S.A. less time is spent in family-related activities than in France. (Turn to p. 92, C)

D.   The girls are homesick for their families. (Turn to p. 95, D)

Sympathiques Nice   **Qu'est-ce que tu veux dire?** What do you mean?

11.   Du Steak à très bon marché °

Food

Dans le couloir ° d'un immeuble à Paris. Jeffrey et Michael viennent de sortir de leur petit appartement.

Jeffrey:	Ce que nous trouvons très cher, madame, c'est la viande.
Mme. Amadou:	Oui, les prix sont très élevés. °
Michael:	(Michael ne parle pas français, mais il le comprend un peu.) Tell her I know a great place to buy steak.
Jeffrey:	Mon camarade vient de me dire ° qu'il sait où on peut acheter du steak à très bon marché. (A Michael) Where is it, Michael?
Michael:	It's six blocks down the street on the left side. You can't miss it. Just look for their sign which is a statue of a horse's head which extends out from the building.
Jeffrey:	C'est une boucherie à six rues d'ici, en descendant l'avenue. Là où il y a une statue de cheval...
Mme. Amadou:	Ah oui, moi aussi, j'y achète parfois de la viande. Mais je préfère le boeuf.
Jeffrey:	Mais c'est très bon. Nous en avons mangé hier soir. °

Why is the meat cheaper at the butcher shop where Michael shops?

A.   It is located in a less affluent neighborhood. (Turn to p. 94, A)
B.   The beef is of an inferior quality. (Turn to p. 92, B)
C.   The horse-head butcher shops are a large chain and can offer lower prices. (Turn to p. 95, C)
D.   Horsemeat is cheaper than beef. (Turn to p. 93, D)

à très bon marché inexpensive   **couloir** hallway   **élevés** high
vient de me dire has just told me
Nous en avons mangé hier soir. We ate some last night.

12.   Mal au foie°

Health, language

Pointe-à-Pitre, Guadeloupe.

Donna: Comment allez-vous, monsieur?
Pierre: Pas très bien, mademoiselle. J'ai mal au foie.
Donna: Oh, j'espère que ce n'est pas trop sérieux.
Pierre: Ce n'est pas très grave. Je m'en remettrai° peut-être.
Donna: (A elle-même) Poor Pierre! He's really sick!

Which of the following choices best describes Pierre's state of health?

A.   He is not sick, but is trying to gain sympathy. (Turn to p. 69, A)
B.   He is not feeling well because of temporary indigestion. (Turn to p. 71, B)
C.   He is very sick and is uncertain about whether or not he will recover. (Turn to p. 59, C)
D.   He has cirrhosis of the liver. (Turn to p. 68, D)

---

foie liver   **je m'en remettrai** I will recover from it

13. En Vacances

Education, leisure-time activities, economy

Charles, un étudiant de Grenoble, passe le mois de juillet chez une famille américaine à San Francisco.

Peter: Je vais finir mon travail à cinq heures. On peut aller se baigner° à cette heure-là, si tu veux.

Charles: D'accord. Je vais en ville pour voir le quartier des quais. Je vais passer au restaurant où tu travailles à quatres heures et demie, et tu vas me vendre un hamburger, n'est-ce pas?

Peter: O.K. . . .Charles, où travailles-tu à Grenoble quand tu ne voyages pas?

Charles: Je travaille beaucoup à mes études.°

Why does Charles not work in France?

A. Charles is not expected to work in France. (Turn to p. 63, A)
B. Charles is lazy. (Turn to p. 53, B)
C. Charles is from a very rich family. (Turn to p. 58, C)
D. Charles does not value the finer things money can buy. (Turn to p. 59, D)

---

se baigner to go swimming   **mes études** my studies

14. Ne Touchez pas aux fruits!

Social proprieties

Un marché aux fruits près du Centre universitaire° à Paris.

Mary: Tiens! Kyung Sook, regarde ces belles pêches!

Kyung Sook: Oui, elles ont l'air délicieux. Achetons des fruits pour le dessert.

Mary: Bonne idée!
(Elles prennent des pêches et les admirent.)

Marchande: (En colère) Mais, que faites-vous, mesdemoiselles?!! Je vous en prie!° Ne touchez pas aux fruits! Vous n'êtes pas chez vous.

Mary: Je viens de perdre° l'appétit. Je ne veux plus de dessert.

Kyung Sook: Moi non plus.° Allons-nous-en.°

Why did the fruit seller become angry?

A. She does not like foreigners. (Turn to p. 58, A)

B. The saleswoman thought the girls were shoplifting. (Turn to p. 60, B)

C. The fruit seller usually handles the fruit for the clients at the markets in France. (Turn to p. 69, C)

D. The fruit seller does not like students. (Turn to p. 53, D)

Centre universitaire University residential center
Je viens de perdre I have just lost
Allons-nous-en Let's leave.

Je vous en prie! Please!
Moi non plus. Me neither.

15.   Quel langage!

Social proprieties, youth culture, intellectuality, language

Au restaurant universitaire. Bordeaux, France.

Françoise: Mon dieu que ce plat est déguelasse! °
Charlene: Quel langage!
Françoise: Ce n'est pas de ma faute si on nous sert ° ces cochonneries. °
                 Je ne peux plus manger.
Charlene: Françoise! Quelle manière de parler!

What is wrong with what Françoise is saying?

A.   She lacks self-control. (Turn to p. 54, A)
B.   The French try to find the positive in things rather than being so
         critical. (Turn to p. 68, B)
C.   She said *mon dieu, déguelasse*, and *cochonneries*. (Turn to p. 55,
         C)
D.   Nothing is wrong; Françoise has said nothing in this situation
         which is inconsistent with the usual manner of talking among
         French teenagers. (Turn to p. 67, D)

---

déguelasse (slang) disgusting
ces cochonneries trashy stuff

on nous sert they serve us

16.   Ma Fête

Religion, joy of life

Pointe-à-Pitre, Guadeloupe.

Shirley: C'est le 4 juin aujourd'hui. C'est mon anniversaire. J'ai dix-huit ans.
Guy: Bon anniversaire, Shirley! Je t'invite à prendre un pot. °
Shirley: Merci, Guy. Et ton anniversaire, c'est quand?
Guy: Mon anniversaire? C'est le 25 septembre. Mais je vais célébrer la Saint Guy la semaine prochaine, le 12 juin. Ce jour-là tu me feras un cadeau, ° si tu veux.
Shirley: Ah oui?

Why is Guy going to celebrate the following week?

A. Guy, being named after Saint Guy, celebrates his saint's day as well as his birthday. (Turn to p. 61, A)
B. As a pretext for a party, Guy makes up a reason for celebrating the following week also. (Turn to p. 54, B)
C. Guy is particularly religious. (Turn to p. 66, C)
D. The French, especially those of Guadeloupe, do not like to be outdone, so Guy wants to have a celebration. (Turn to p. 71, D)

---

prendre un pot   to have a glass (of wine, beer, coke, etc.)
tu me feras un cadeau   You can give me a present

16

17. Au Deuxième étage?

Housing, language

Au bureau de tabac. Québec, Canada.

Paul: Pardon, monsieur. S'il vous plaît, où est le bureau de tourisme?

Marchand: C'est en face, au deuxième étage.

Paul: Merci, monsieur. Au revoir, monsieur.

Marchand: Je vous en prie. Au revoir, monsieur.
(Dix minutes plus tard, Paul retourne au bureau de tabac pour acheter une revue.)

Paul: Monsieur, vous m'avez dit que le bureau de tourisme est au deuxième étage, mais, en réalité, c'est au troisième étage.

Marchand: (En riant) Ah, mais non, monsieur. Vous vous trompez.° Comme je vous ai dit,° le bureau de tourisme est au deuxième étage. Allez-y.° Vous allez voir.

Paul: (A lui-même) Ce marchand se moque de moi.°

What is the reason for the above conflict?

A. Paul has no sense of humor. (Turn to p. 73, A)
B. The "third" floor in English is actually the "second" floor in French. (Turn to p. 74, B)
C. The tobacconist was purposefully giving Paul the wrong directions. (Turn to p. 75, C)
D. Paul went up two floors and thought he had gone up three floors. (Turn to p. 74, D)

étage floor
Comme je vous ai dit As I told you
se moque de moi is making fun of me

Vous vous trompez. You are making a mistake.
Allez-y. Go there.

18. Ces Cafés sont bondés!°

Common sense, leisure-time activities

Un couple américain parle avec un couple allemand pendant une excursion à Paris.

Mme. White: Regardez tous ces restaurants avec des terrasses.

M. Schultz: Oui, et ils sont tous bondés.

Mme. White: Il semble que les Français passent beaucoup de temps dans les cafés.

M. Schultz: Oui, on m'a dit qu'on peut passer des heures dans un café sans qu'on vous dise de vous en aller.°

Mme. White: Oui, je comprends. Ici il y a une façon de penser différente. Aux Etats-Unis on est plus travailleur. On ne perd pas son temps dan les cafés.

Why are the terraces of the cafés full?

A. The French waste a lot of time in cafés. (Turn to p. 77, A)

B. Most of the people on the terraces of cafés are foreigners. (Turn to p. 76, B)

C. The French pride themselves in their ability to relax when it is time to relax and work when it is time to work. (Turn to p. 78, C)

D. Most of the people in the cafés are actually working. (Turn to p. 79, D)

---

bondés overflowing
sans qu'on vous dise de vous en aller and no one will tell you to leave

18

19. Le Bac

Education, social stratification

Bill parle avec Odile, une étudiante française de Guadeloupe qui passe ses vacances chez une famille américaine. Bill parle de son amie Hélène, sa correspondante française qui vient de lui envoyer° une lettre. Chicago, Illinois.

Bill: Comme vous, Odile, Hélène a dix-huit ans.
Odile: Où est-ce qu'elle habite?
Bill: Elle habite Chalon-en-Bourgogne près de Lyon.
Odile: Comment la trouvez-vous?
Bill: Ah, elle est très sympathique. Mais je crois qu'elle n'est pas très intelligente. Elle m'a écrit qu'elle a été refusée à° son baccalauréat. Et elle n'avait pas honte° de me le dire.°
Odile: Ah, oui?

Why did Hélène fail the baccalaureate exam?

A. The exam was very difficult. (Turn to p. 66, A)
B. Since she went to a lycée in a small town, her teachers were not very good. (Turn to p. 70, B)
C. Her teachers expected too much of her. (Turn to p. 54, C)
D. She's not very intelligent. (Turn to p. 63, D)

---

qui vient de lui envoyer   who has just sent him
elle a été refusée à   she failed   **elle n'avait pas honte**   she wasn't ashamed
de me le dire   to tell me about it

20.   Des Capitalistes américains

Intellectuality, individualism, social proprieties

A la terrasse d'un café à Paris.

Henri: Les Américains ont versé° des milliers de litres de pétrole dans l'océan.

Jeanne: Oui, moi aussi, j'ai lu cela dans *Le Monde* hier soir. C'est très bête,° n'est-ce pas? On gâche° tout dans la nature.

Harvey: Oui, c'est un désastre. Je le regrette beaucoup.

Henri: Ce sont des capitalistes américains qui ne se préoccupent pas° du monde qu'ils détruisent.

Jeanne: Oui, et pendant que leurs bateaux de pétrole détruisent l'océan, leurs usines polluent l'atmosphère jusqu'à ce que° nous ne puissions plus respirer.°

Harvey: Oui, vous avez raison. J'ai honte° d'être américain.

Why did Harvey's answer disappoint the French students?

A. They were waiting for Harvey to "defend" his country against their exaggerations. (Turn to p. 97, A)

B. They felt sorry for him because he is an American. (Turn to p. 96, B)

C. They did not think he was sincerely ashamed. (Turn to p. 98, C)

D. They thought that he was an American capitalist. (Turn to p. 99, D)

---

ont versé have poured out   **bête** stupid   **On gâche** They ruin
qui ne se préoccupent pas who don't have worry about
jusqu'à ce que until   **nous ne puissions plus respirer** we can no longer breathe
J'ai honte I am ashamed

21. Un Peu bourgeoise

Language, social proprieties

Françoise vient de quitter Ellen et Jacqueline. Dans un café, Fort-de-France, Martinique.

Ellen:	Tu connais Françoise depuis longtemps?
Jacqueline:	Oui, assez longtemps. Nous étions° au même lycée.° Elle est un peu bourgeoise, tu ne trouves pas?
Ellen:	Ah oui, je crois qu'elle est de la bourgeoisie.
Jacqueline:	Je veux dire qu'elle parle un peu trop de ses achats, combien elle a payé ceci, combien elle a payé cela.
Ellen:	Oui, ce n'est pas amusant de toujours parler d'argent. Dis, Jacqueline, la plupart des Français sont de la bourgeoisie, n'est-ce pas?
Jacqueline:	Oui, je me souviens de° ce que nous a dit notre professeur° d'histoire: la bourgeoisie est assez grande en France, mais elle l'est encore plus° aux Etats-Unis.

Why does Ellen not understand Jacqueline?

A. She does not understand French class structure. (Turn to p. 100, A)

B. She does not know the characteristics of the bourgeoisie. (Turn to p. 100, B)

C. She does not realize that *bourgeois* can have more than one meaning. (Turn to p. 102, C)

D. She does not realize that the class structure is not the same in France as it is in the United States. (Turn to p. 101, D)

Nous étions We were **au même lycée** at the same secondary school
je me souviens de I remember
ce que nous a dit notre professeur what our teacher told us
l'est encore plus is even more so

22. Les Ivrognes

Social proprieties, common sense

Le 14 juillet Jake et Patty traversent la France en auto. Ils s'arrêtent°
pour prendre un café dans un restaurant. Tours, France.

Jake: Il y a beaucoup de monde dans la rue.
Le garçon: Oui, bien sûr. Il est difficile de conduire. Les rues principales sont bouchées.°
Patty: En entrant dans le café des jeunes gens nous ont un peu bousculés.° Ils ont trop bu,° je crois.
Le garçon: Sans doute. Ils s'amusent. Mais ils ne font pas de mal, n'est-ce pas?
Patty: Non. (A son mari) Gosh, there seem to be a lot of drunks in France.

Why are there tipsy people in the street?

A. The water not being good, the people are forced to drink wine. (Turn to p. 68, A)
B. The French drink too much wine with their meals. (Turn to p. 69, B)
C. Only on rare, special occasions do the French drink to excess. (Turn to p. 71, C)
D. French wine has a very high alcohol content. (Turn to p. 61, D)

Ils s'arrêtent They stop   **bouchées** congested
bousculés bumped against   **Ils ont trop bu** They've drunk too much

23. C'est déguelasse!

Food, common sense

Guillaume et Jeanne passent un mois chez des familles américaines près de New York.

Jeanne: Tu étais° malade la semaine passée, n'est-ce pas? Ça va mieux?

Guillaume: Oui, merci. Je vais mieux maintenant. Ta famille américaine mange-t-elle autant de boîtes de conserve° que la mienne?°

Jeanne: Peut-être bien. Les légumes frais me manquent beaucoup.° Ceux des boîtes de conserve n'ont pas de goût, n'est-ce pas?

Guillaume: Non, pas du tout. Et ils mettent tant de produits chimiques dans leurs aliments pour les conserver. Sur le paquet de pain il est indiqué: "calcium proprionate added to retard spoilage". Le bon pain frais me manque beaucoup.

Jeanne: Oui, et c'est déguelasse° ce qu'ils mangent au petit déjeuner. Sur les cartons il est indiqué: "BHT added to retard spoilage".

Guillaume: Aux Etats-Unis on doit faire attention à ce qu'on mange.

Why are these French people so suspicious of American food?

A. The international reputation of American food is not quite as high as the reputation of French food. (Turn to p. 71, A)

B. The French students miss French cooking. (Turn to p. 56, B)

C. The French are generally suspicious of processed and artificially preserved food. (Turn to p. 70, C)

D. The French students are fussy about what they eat, because they have been babied too much. (Turn to p. 69, D)

Tu étais You were   **boîtes de conserve** canned goods   **la mienne** mine
Les légumes frais me manquent beaucoup. I miss fresh vegetables a lot.
déguelasse disgusting

24. L'Etudiant en France

Education, leisure-time activities

Dans un café près du lycée. Fort-de-France, Martinique.

Etienne: Alors, vous êtes venue en groupe à la Martinique de votre high school?

Amy: Oui. Monsieur Johnson, le conseiller de notre club de français a organisé ce voyage pour nous. Nous nous amusons beaucoup dans notre club de français et nous y apprenons beaucoup aussi.

Etienne: Ce monsieur est votre professeur et aussi le conseiller de votre club?

Amy: Vous trouvez ça bizarre? Vous avez un club d'anglais dans votre lycée, n'est-ce pas?

Etienne: Non, les lycées français n'ont pas de clubs.

Amy: Alors, que faites-vous après les classes?

Etienne: Nous rentrons chez nous. D'habitude nous ne sortons pas du lycée avant cinq heures de l'après-midi.

Amy: Et puis, le soir vous sortez parfois?

Etienne: Rarement. Il y a beaucoup de devoirs à faire presque tous les soirs.

Amy: Ce n'est pas drôle d'être étudiant en France.

Etienne: Ce n'est pas si mal.

Why does Amy consider student life so serious in France?

A.   The students remain at school late each day. (Turn to p. 89, A)
B.   Amy is a rather lazy student. (Turn to p. 88, B)
C.   Etienne is exaggerating the amount of homework in France. (Turn to p. 90, C)
D.   French students have few recreational activities sponsored by the lycée. (Turn to p. 91, D)

24

25. Des Grilles

Housing, individualism, family life

Jane, américaine, et Freda, allemande, travaillent au pair ° chez des familles françaises. Tours, France.

Jane: Avez-vous remarqué que les Français ont très souvent des murs, des arbres, et des arbustes ° autour de leurs maisons?

Freda: Oui, je l'ai remarqué, moi aussi. Et certaines maisons ont des grilles d'entrée. °

Jane: Oui, et les marchands ont aussi des barrières qu'ils mettent la nuit à leurs portes et à leurs vitrines. °

Freda: Je suppose qu'ils ont peur des voleurs, ° donc, ils se protègent.

Jane: Ça fait peur de voir tous les murs et les grilles.

Why do the French prefer walls, fences, and vegetation around their houses?

A.   They like privacy. (Turn to p. 86, A)
B.   They feel that it beautifies the home. (Turn to p. 84, B)
C.   They are all required by law to have walls. (Turn to p. 86, C)
D.   They put up barriers to keep out criminals. (Turn to p. 85, D)

---

au pair   for board, loding, and a little spending money
grilles d'entrée   wrought-iron entrance gates
voleurs   robbers

arbustes   bushes
vitrines   shop windows

26. En brique

Housing, social proprieties

Hélène, étudiante française, passe un mois chez les Brown à Cincinnati aux Etats-Unis.

Mme. Brown: Oui, nous aimons bien notre petite maison. Roger passe tout son temps à bricoler,° à peindre, et à faire des réparations.

Hélène: Les Français préfèrent les maisons construites en brique ou en pierre. Ça dure plus longtemps.

Mme. Brown: Ah bon? (Hélène sort.)

Mme. Brown: Roger, I don't know why she had to say that the French like houses made of brick, when she knows that our house is made of wood.

M. Brown: I guess that means she doesn't like our house. I wonder if she doesn't like our food too. How ungrateful can you get!

Why did Hélène say that the French prefer brick houses when she was a guest in the Browns' wooden home?

A. In conversation, some French people are often more eager to express the truth than they are concerned about injuring the sensitivities of others. (Turn to p. 85, A)

B. The French are very insensitive people. (Turn to p. 86, B)

C. Hélène does not appreciate what the Browns have done for her. (Turn to p. 84, C)

D. Hélène actually does not like the Browns. (Turn to p. 87, D)

---

bricoler to putter

27.   Lequel °est le professeur?

Education

Dans la cour de récréation d'un lycée. Lille, France.

Joyce: Alors, les lycées n'ont pas d'équipes° sportives comme les écoles secondaires aux Etats-Unis.

M. Renard: Non, mademoiselle. Il y a des cours d'éducation physique, bien sûr, mais nous ne voyons pas l'organisation des équipes sportives comme un des buts° de notre système d'éducation.

Joyce: Tiens! C'est un professeur d'éducation physique, n'est-ce pas? Il a l'air aussi jeune que certains de ces étudiants.

M. Renard: Mademoiselle, c'est un surveillant. Il contrôle les allées et venues° des jeunes et les empêche° de courir et de se bousculer° dans les couloirs.

Joyce: Ah oui, je comprends. Aux Etats-Unis nous appelons cela *hall duty*. (A elle-même) Il est tout de même° très jeune pour être professeur.

What is a surveillant?

A.   The *surveillant* is a teacher on hall duty. (Turn to p. 80, A)
B.   The *surveillant* is one of the older lycée students. (Turn to p. 82, B)
C.   The *surveillant* is a physical education teacher. (Turn to p. 81, C)
D.   The *surveillant* is a university student working part-time at a lycée. (Turn to p. 72, D)

Lequel Which one   **équipes** teams   **buts** goals
Les allées et venues the comings and goings   **empêche** prevents
se bousculer to bump each other   **tout de même** even so

28.   Sympathiques...mais pressés

Social proprieties, leisure-time activities

Monsieur et Madame Wolinski, Américains, viennent de sortir de chez les Tardier où ils étaient invités à dîner avec six autres invités. Voilà une conversation entre l'hôtesse,° Madame Tardier, et Madame Carnot au sujet des Wolinski.

Mme. Tardier: Ils sont sympathiques, ces Américains, n'est-ce pas?
Mme. Carnot: Oui, assez. Mais ils semblaient pressés, comme d'autres Américains que je connais.
Mme. Tardier: Comment pressés?
Mme. Carnot: Ils étaient les premiers à partir.
Mme. Tardier: Cela n'a pas d'importance. On peut partir quand on veut.
Mme. Carnot: Et puis, ils n'ont pas pris le temps de nous quitter très aimablement.
Mme. Tardier: Au moins,° ils ont crié: "Au revoir tout le monde" avant de partir.
Mme. Carnot: Oui, c'est tout ce qu'ils ont fait.

According to French etiquette, what should the Wolinskis have done?

A.   They should have been nicer. (Turn to p. 99, A)
B.   They should not have been in such a hurry. (Turn to p. 97, B)
C.   They should have shook the hand of every person in attendance. (Turn to p. 99, C)
D.   They should have been the last to leave. (Turn to p. 98, D)

---

l'hôtesse   the hostess

au moins   at least

29.   La Sortie

Youth culture, social proprieties

David a fait la connaissance de Marie-Claude et de plusieurs autres étudiants qui déjeunent ensemble au Mabillon, restaurant universitaire à Paris.

Marie-Claude: Viens voir Ferrat ce soir. Il va chanter à l'Olympia. On va se réunir° à sept heures devant le Mabillon, et on va y aller en métro, ça va?

David: Bon, si tu veux. Pourquoi pas? Formidable! A ce soir à sept heures, Marie-Claude.

Marie-Claude: A ce soir. Bon appétit, mon vieux. Ciao!° (Marie-Claude sort. Jean-Paul entre.)

Jean-Paul: Bonjour David. Tu as l'air heureux. Qu'est-ce qui t'est arrivé?°

David: C'est que. . .je ne sais pas. . .c'est que je vais sortir avec une camarade française ce soir. Et ce qui m'étonne,° c'est elle qui m'a invité à sortir. Moi, je ne l'ai pas invitée.

What did Marie-Claude want to communicate to David?

A.   The whole group of friends would be waiting at the Mabillon to go to the Olympia all together. (Turn to p. 64, A)

B.   She liked David a lot. (Turn to p. 58, B)

C.   In France girls often ask fellows for dates. (Turn to p. 57, C)

D.   She would be waiting for him to pick her up at her home at 7 p.m. (Turn to p. 54, D)

---

se réunir to meet   **Ciao!** Good-bye
Qu'est-ce qui t'est arrivé? What happened to you?
ce qui m'étonne what astonishes me

29

30. Elle ne parle pas

Individualism, liberty

Betty travaille au pair° chez la famille Foucart. Angers, France.

Mme. Foucart: Que pensez-vous du dîner? Il vous a plu?°
Betty: Oui, madame.
Mme. Foucart: Est-ce qu'on sert de la sauce hollandaise aux Etats-Unis aussi?
Betty: Oui, madame.
M. Foucart: Betty, que pensez-vous des élections aux Etats-Unis?
Betty: C'est intéressant.
M. Foucart: Qui sera élu,° un démocrate ou un républicain, d'après vous?
Betty: Un démocrate, je crois. . .Excusez-moi, je vais dans ma chambre faire mes devoirs. (Elle sort.)
M. Foucart: L'Américaine, elle fait assez bien le ménage,° mais elle n'a pas grand-chose à nous dire, n'est-ce pas?
Mme. Foucart: Non, c'est vrai. Elle est sympathique, mais très timide. timide.

What is the reason for the slightly strained relationship between Betty and the Foucarts?

A. They do not like her. (Turn to p. 60, A)
B. She does not talk with them. (Turn to p. 62, B)
C. She does not like them. (Turn to p. 63, C)
D. They do not agree politically. (Turn to p. 64, D)

---

au pair for board, lodging, and a little spending money
Il vous a plu? Did you like it?   **Qui sera élu?** Who will be elected?
le ménage the housework

31. Les Enfants boivent.°...

Food, family

Deux Américains avec un Français dans un restaurant. Grenoble, France.

M. Rizotto: Le coq au vin° est vraiment savoureux. Vous ne trouvez pas?

M. Blondel: Oui, je suis content d'avoir commandé le coq au vin, moi aussi.

Mme. Rizotto: Vous avez très bien choisi le vin, Georges. Il est formidable.

M. Rizotto: A propos de ça,° regardez ces enfants à la table à côté qui boivent aussi du vin. On commence à boire du vin assez jeune en France, n'est-ce pas?

Mme. Rizotto: C'est étonnant! On ne devrait pas° laisser boire les enfants.

M. Blondel: Un peu de vin ne va pas leur faire de mal.

Why are these French children drinking wine?

A. The French are careless in the raising of their children. (Turn to p. 76, A)
B. It is not really wine that they are drinking. (Turn to p. 77, B)
C. The French have looser morals than Americans. (Turn to p. 79, C)
D. French children are served very little wine, not enough to hurt them. (Turn to p. 78, D)

---

boivent drink
A propos de ça Speaking of that
Le coq au vin Chicken cooked in wine

32. La Saleté °

Ecology, cleanliness

Anne, une jeune Française, passe un mois chez une famille américaine près de Boston.

Anne: Que c'est sale! ° Je ne savais pas. °
Johnny: Qu'est-ce qui est sale? Je ne vois rien. . .
Anne: Les rues sont sales. Regarde tous ces papiers.
Johnny: C'est curieux. Tu me dis que Boston est sale. Et Patricia Martin, qui vient de visiter Paris avec ses parents, m'a dit que Paris est sale.
Anne: Ce n'est pas vrai. Paris est propre. °

What is the reason for the conflicting opinions concerning the cleanliness of Paris and Boston?

A. Anne is too proud to admit that Paris is dirty. (Turn to p. 78, A)
B. What people consider dirty in one country is not necessarily dirty in another. (Turn to p. 79, B)
C. Johnny is too proud to admit that Boston is a dirty city. (Turn to p. 77, C)
D. Anne does not like Boston. (Turn to p. 76, D)

La Saleté Dirtiness
Je ne savais pas. I didn't know.

sale dirty
propre clean

33. Chacun° paie sa part

Youth culture, social proprieties

Près de l'université. Dijon, France.

Arnold: Avez-vous jamais vu "La Dolce Vita"?

Jacqueline: Non, je ne l'ai jamais vu mais je voudrais le voir.

Arnold: Je sais qu'on le repasse actuellement° dans un des cinémas du quartier. Ecoutez! J'ai une idée. Je voudrais voir ce film, moi aussi. Voulez-vous m'accompagner? Nous pourrons y aller maintenant, à la séance de quatre heures, si vous êtes libre.

Jacqueline: Je ne sais pas. . .Bon alors. Pourquoi pas? Allons-y. (Au guichet Arnold paie les deux billets.)

Jacqueline: Ah, mais non! Vous n'auriez pas dû° payer mon billet. Chacun paie sa part. Tenez!° (Elle met rapidement son argent dans la poche du manteau d'Arnold.)

Arnold: (A lui-même) Elle est ingrate° de ne pas apprécier ce que je voulais faire pour elle.

Why did Jacqueline act as she did?

A. Jacqueline does not know how to act on a date. (Turn to p. 75; A)
B. French people always like to pay their own way. (Turn to p. 80, B)
C. Jacqueline is ungrateful. (Turn to p. 74, C)
D. French students usually pay their own way. (Turn to p. 73, D)

Chacun Each one   **ingrate** ungrateful   **actuellement** now
Vous n'auriez pas dû You shouldn't have
Tenez! Take it!

34. On s'embrasse°

Family, social proprieties

Dans un compartiment du train de Paris, dans la gare de Lyon.

Eddie: Regardez, Françoise. Voilà le garçon dont vous avez parlé. Il est descendu du train.

Françoise: Oui, il paraît° qu'il habite Lyon. Il cherche quelqu'un.

James: Oui, regardez, il s'approche de° ce vieux monsieur. Son père, sans doute.

Eddie: Mon Dieu!! Vous avez vu ce qu'ils ont fait!! Ils se sont embrassés!

James: C'est étonnant! En public comme ça.

Françoise: Qu'est-ce qu'il y a d'extraordinaire?

Françoise reacted differently from the American boys. Why?

A. In France it is normal for a father and a son to embrace. (Turn to p. 72, A)

B. Françoise is acting as if she had not seen the men embrace. (Turn to p. 73, B)

C. Françoise is acting blasé and worldly, as if she were not surprised. (Turn to p. 80, C)

D. The French have looser morals than Americans. (Turn to p. 75, D)

On s'embrasse They embrace (or kiss)   **il paraît** it seems

35. Cette drôle de dame°

Family, individualism

Dans le métro à Paris.

Mary: Look at that cute little boy sitting with his mother across from us. Isn't he just darling! (Smiling broadly, Mary waves at the little boy.) Bonjour! Bonjour! Bonjour! Bonjour!

Le garçon: (Sérieux) Maman, regarde ce que fait cette drôle de dame. Elle est drôle, n'est-ce pas?

La mère: Oui, mon enfant.

Why didn't the little boy and his mother appreciate Mary's attentions?

A. Mary likes little children more than usual. (Turn to p. 84, A)

B. The little boy is overly serious and grown-up for his age. (Turn to p. 87, B)

C. In France cute little children are not used to getting attention from strangers. (Turn to p. 85, C)

D. French people do not appreciate little children. (Turn to p. 86, D)

Cette drôle de dame That funny (strange) lady

36.   La Télévision

Intellectuality, communications

Claude fait un voyage aux Etats-Unis. Seattle, Washington.

Claude: C'est une perte° de temps, regarder la télévision américaine.

Ronald: Pourquoi dites-vous cela?

Claude: Il semble° qu'il y a plus de temps consacré à la publicité qu'aux programmes. Au moment où le programme devient intéressant, on l'arrête et on présente encore de la publicité. C'est très ennuyeux.°

Ronald: On finit par s'habituer à° tant de publicité.

Claude: Pas moi! Et les programmes sont bêtes. Hier soir, j'ai mis beaucoup de chaînes, et il n'y avait rien de vraiment intéressant.

Ronald: On a des programmes pour des goûts différents. Avez-vous regardé l'horaire des programmes? Il y a des chaînes qui n'ont pas de publicité, celles qui ont des programmes éducatifs.

Claude: Hier soir, j'ai mis plusieurs chaînes, et il y avait toujours de la publicité et des programmes bêtes.

What does Claude not seem to understand about American television?

A. American television does not really have many advertisements. (Turn to p. 96, A)

B. Educational channels are somewhat similar to French television in programming and limited advertisements. (Turn to p. 98, B)

C. American television programs are usually of high educational value. (Turn to p. 96, C)

D. In France advertisements do not interrupt programs, but are placed at the beginning and at the end of each program. (Turn to p. 97, D)

---

perte loss   **Il semble** It seems   **ennuyeux** aggravating
On finit par s'habituer à You finally get used to

37. L'Auto-stop°

Individualism, family

Jeffrey fait de l'auto-stop avec un Belge, Jean-Paul. Au bord de la route dans la banlieue° près d'Orléans, France.

Jean-Paul: Cela fait deux bonnes heures que nous attendons ici et personne ne s'arrête.

Jeffrey: Oui, c'est curieux. En Angleterre et en Allemagne d'habitude je n'attendais guère plus de dix minutes avant d'être pris. Je ne le comprends pas.

Jean-Paul: Ecoute, Jeffrey, il vaut mieux te débarrasser du° drapeau américain que tu as mis sur tes bagages pour attirer les automobilistes.

Jeffrey: Ah bon? Tu as peut-être raison. Je croyais que les Français aimaient les Américains.

Why didn't anyone stop to pick up the two boys?

A. Because of the location of the two boys on the highway, it would have been difficult for cars to stop. (Turn to p. 55, A)
B. The French consider hitchhikers as bums. (Turn to p. 65, B)
C. The French are suspicious of strangers. (Turn to p. 61, C)
D. The French do not like Americans. (Turn to p. 58, D)

L'auto-stop Hitchhiking   **la banlieue** the suburbs
il vaut mieux te débarrasser de it would be better to get rid of

38.   Origine paysanne

Social stratification, minorities

John est assistant d'anglais dans un lycée. Il parle avec Sara, jeune professeur d'histoire. Paris, France.

Sara:	John, vous m'avez dit que vos grands-parents ont émigré de la Pologne aux Etats-Unis.
John:	Oui, c'était avant la Grande Guerre.
Sara:	Qu'est-ce qu'ils faisaient vos grands-parents, là-bas en Pologne?
John:	Ils étaient enfants quand ils ont émigré, mais je crois que leurs parents étaient fermiers.
Sara:	Tiens!° Tiens! Alors, vous êtes d'origine paysanne!

Why was Sara astonished by John's background?

A.   Sara has prejudices against Polish people. (Turn to p. 59, A)
B.   Sara has prejudices against farmers. (Turn to p. 63, B)
C.   It is more difficult to change social classes in France than in the United States. (Turn to p. 56, C)
D.   In France a person is considered a reflection of the low class of his or her ancestors on the father's side even if he or she becomes well-educated and rich. (Turn to p. 55, D)

Tiens!   Well!

39. Le Langage des fleurs

Social proprieties, language, family

Jane a été invitée chez les Bertrand, dont la fille Jacqueline est une de ses camarades. Nantes, France.

Mme. Bertrand: Ah, bonjour, mademoiselle. Entrez. Je suis contente que vous soyez venue° dîner avec nous.

Jane: Bonjour, madame Bertrand. Je suis heureuse de faire votre connaissance. (Elle lui tend° des fleurs.)

Mme. Bertrand: Des roses! Oh, vous n'auriez pas dû!° Je suis gênée.°

Jane: Je m'excuse, madame. Je croyais qu'il faut apporter des fleurs quand on est invité chez quelqu'un en France.

Which alternative best explains this conflict?

A. Jane brought the wrong kind of flowers. (Turn to p. 67, A)
B. Jane should have brought candy instead of flowers. (Turn to p. 59, B)
C. Jane misunderstood madame Bertrand, who liked flowers. (Turn to p. 68, C)
D. Jane should not have brought flowers. (Turn to p. 70, D)

---

soyez venue have come
vous n'auriez pas dû you shouldn't have

Elle lui tend She extends to her
gênée embarrassed

40.   Qu'est-ce que c'est?

Travel, housing

A l'Hôtel du Gros Lion. Paris, France.

Mme. Wenstrom: Oh, what a beautiful room! Do you like it, David?

M. Wenstrom: Yes, look at the great view. You can see that big, famous white church. What's it called? Monsieur, comment s'appelle cette église?

Le portier: C'est le Sacré Cœur, monsieur. La chambre vous plaît?° C'est très bien.

Mme. Wenstrom: (From the bathroom) My goodness, David, what's this thing? And there's no shower, not even a tub.

M. Wenstrom: I don't know. Monsieur, qu'est-ce que c'est que cette chose-là?

Le portier: Ça, c'est le bidet.

M. Wenstrom: Que faut-il faire avec un bidet?

Le portier: Vous plaisantez,° Monsieur. On se lave avec le bidet.

M. Wenstrom: Et la douche?° (Il se fâche. °) On m'a menti. ° On vient de me dire en bas que cet hôtel a des douches.

Le portier: Bien sûr, monsieur. Nous avons des douches. Il y a une douche à chaque étage au bout du° couloir.

What is the reason for the conflict?

A. The hotel management has been dishonest by telling lies to Mr. Wenstrom. (Turn to p. 74, A)

B. The hotel management has given their worst room to the Wenstroms. (Turn to p. 75, B)

C. The bathroom with toilet, sink, and bidet (with a community shower) is considered sufficient in France. (Turn to p. 73, C)

D. The French are not as clean as the Americans. (Turn to p. 80, D)

La chambre vous plaît? Do you like the room?
la douche   the shower
On a menti.   They lied.

Vous plaisantez   You're joking
Il se fâche.   He becomes angry.
au bout du   at the end of

41. Le Chahut°

Individualism, education

Jenifer est assistante d'anglais dans un lycée. Elle raconte° à Horst, l'assistant d'allemand, ce qu'elle a vu dans une des classes d'anglais de Madame Levallois. Nice, France.

Jenifer: Tu sais, Madame Levallois est forte° comme prof. Mais elle ne réussit pas toujours à faire taire° les étudiants.

Horst: Qu'est-ce qu'elle a fait, ou n'a pas fait, pour te donner cette impression?

Jenifer: Tout au commencement elle s'est mise à° parler à la classe. Moi, je n'ai rien compris à ces premières phrases, tant les gosses° faisaient du bruit. Puis, ils se sont tus° subitement.° Un peu plus tard, ils ont soudainement chahuté et, peu après,° ils se sont tus.

What would you conclude from Jenifer's observations?

A. Nothing happened that would indicate that Madame Levallois could not control the students. (Turn to p. 79, A)

B. American teachers in general are stronger disciplinarians than French teachers. (Turn to p. 78, B)

C. French students don't generally respect their teachers. (Turn to p. 76, C)

D. Madame Levallois tried but could not keep the students quiet. (Turn to p. 77, D)

Le chahut Uproar (of students)
forte strong (qualified)
elle s'est mise à she began to
ils se sont tus they became quiet
peu après soon afterward

raconte relates
faire taire to quiet
les gosses the kids
subitement very quickly

42. On m'a collé!°

Transportation

Clermont-Ferrand, France.

Charles: Suzanne, Jacqueline et moi, nous allons au cinéma cet après-midi. Tu veux nous accompagner?

Jean-Paul: Malheureusement, je ne peux pas. Je vais passer° un examen à l'Auto-Ecole à quatre heures.

Charles: Mais, il y a un mois tu m'as dit que tu allais le passer à ce moment-là, en avril.

Jean-Paul: Je l'ai bien passé en avril, mais malheureusement, on m'a collé.

Charles: Si je me souviens° bien, tu m'avais dit en avril que tu avais déjà échoué° une fois. Donc, maintenant, tu as échoué deux fois?

Jean-Paul: Oui, c'est ça. Mais pourquoi tu trouves ça si bizarre? pouvoir te donner encore des leçons.

Why has Jean-Paul already failed the exam twice?

A. Jean-Paul is not very intelligent. (Turn to p. 101, A)

B. The driver-training schools in France fail their students in order to earn more money by giving them more lessons. (Turn to p. 102, B)

C. The French government driver's examinations are very difficult. (Turn to p. 101, C)

D. Jean-Paul needs more practice in driving. (Turn to p. 100, D)

On m'a collé! They failed me! **passer** to take (an exam)
je me souviens I remember **tu y avais déjà échoué** you had already failed it

43. T'es fou° et sais pas conduire!°

Individualism, transportation

Après les vacances. Rouen, France.

Serge: Comme je t'ai dit, mon père, ma mère et moi, nous étions dans notre 304° en Touraine. Il y avait un gars° derrière nous qui trouvait que nous roulions trop lentement. Il a klaxonné° plusieurs fois. Eh bien, ça a irrité mon père, et il a ralenti.°

Douglas: Qu'est-ce qu'il a fait alors, le type derrière vous?

Serge: Il a tâché de nous doubler.° Mais nous avons accéléré pour l'empêcher.° Quand il nous a doublé enfin, il nous a fait un geste° qui a fâché encore plus mon père.

Douglas: Quelle sorte de geste?

Serge: C'était un geste comme s'il voulait dire: "Tu es fou et tu ne sais pas conduire."

Douglas: Qu'est-ce que ton père a fait ensuite?

Serge: Mon père a tâché de doubler le type, mais il a accéléré et a ralenti pour nous gêner.

Douglas: C'est très dangereux ce que faisaient ton père et le type.

Serge: Tu parles!° A un certain moment, nous avons failli° rentrer dans la nature.° Ma mère était tellement bouleversée° qu'elle s'est mise à pleurer. Mon père aussi était bouleversé mais il ne voulait pas l'avouer.

How would you explain this manner of driving?

A. Some French people express their individualism in their manner of driving. (Turn to p. 81, A)

B. French people do not know how to drive well. (Turn to p. 72, B)

C. The French have a lot of fun driving. (Turn to p. 83, C)

D. Passing in France is dangerous. (Turn to p. 82, D)

T'es fou Tu es fou   **sais pas conduire** tu ne sais pas conduire
304 Peugeot model 304 automobile   **un gars** (slang) a guy
klaxonner to honk   **il a ralenti** he slowed down   **doubler** to pass
empêcher to prevent   **geste** gesture   **Tu parles!** That's for sure!
nous avons failli we almost   **rentrer dans la nature** (slang) to go off the road
bouleversée shook up

44. Il ne faut pas resquiller!°

Individualism, leisure-time activities

Dans la queue,° devant le guichet,° une demi-heure avant la présentation à la Comédie Française, à Paris.

Jules:	Nous sommes arrivés assez tôt pour avoir de bonnes places dans la queue. C'est bien, nous aurons de bonnes places.
Doris:	Ah, j'en suis contente. J'aime bien cette pièce. Je crois qu'on a ouvert le guichet. La queue commence à bouger. (Un homme se précipite à une position près du guichet.)
Un monsieur:	Eh?! Que faites-vous la?! Il ne faut pas resquiller! Allez au bout de la queue!
Le resquilleur:	Ne vous énervez pas,° monsieur. Ma femme m'a réservé la place.
Un monsieur:	Moi, je n'ai pas de femme ici pour me réserver une place. Allez au bout de la queue, je vous dis!

Why did the man get so excited?

A. French people get excited about the smallest things. (Turn to p. 82, A)

B. The *resquilleur* had made up a story that his wife was saving him a place. (Turn to p. 81, B)

C. In France people often defend their places in line if someone tries to get ahead of them. (Turn to p. 72, C)

D. The man was ill-tempered. (Turn to p. 83, D)

---

resquiller   to cut in line   **queue**   line
guichet   ticket window   **Ne vous énervez pas**   Don't get angry

45. Les Pauvres enfants

Family, common sense, education

Joe étudie l'art à Paris. Un de ses camarades de classe, Jean-Paul Petit, l'a invité à dîner chez lui. A table il y a les parents de Jean-Paul, son petit frère Pierre, 10 ans, sa petite soeur, 8 ans, et bien entendu, Jean-Paul et Joe. Ils viennent de finir le dessert.

M. Petit: Bon. On avait de la bonne cuisine et de la bonne conversation.

Joe: Je suis très reconnaissant° d'avoir été invité chez vous ce soir. Je comprends maintenant pourquoi la France a une si bonne réputation quand il s'agit de° la cuisine.

Jean-Paul: La cuisine seulement? (On rit.)

Joe: L'art, la littérature, la philosophie, la musique. (On rit.)

Mme. Petit: Il faut bien dire "l'art", n'est-ce pas? Nous sommes parmi° des artistes ce soir. (On rit.)

Pierre: Excusez-moi, mon père, j'ai des devoirs à faire. Je peux aller dans ma chambre?

Marie-Hélène: Moi aussi, papa, s'il te plaît.

M. Petit: Bon, les enfants. Mais, d'abord aidez un peu votre mère dans la cuisine.

Joe: (A lui-même) Il semble qu'on ne laisse pas parler les enfants en France. On est sévère envers° ces pauvres gosses.° Ils n'ont guère° parlé pendant tout le repas.

Why didn't Pierre and Marie-Hélène talk more?

A. In France children are trained to be very polite at the table, to talk very little, and to not interrupt others. (Turn to p. 83, A)

B. The Petit children live in a very authoritarian home where the father is a tyrant. (Turn to p. 83, B)

C. In France children are never allowed to speak at the table. (Turn to p. 82, C)

D. Pierre and Marie-Hélène had just been punished before Joe arrived and were moping. (Turn to p. 81, D)

---

reconnaissant grateful
parmi among
gosses (slang) kids

quand il s'agit de where it is a question of
envers toward
guère scarcely

45

46. Où sont leurs maîtres?°

Animals, family

C'est le trois août. Mary travaille au pair chez les Duval dans une banlieue de Paris. A l'entrée du supermarché.

Mary:	Tenez, regardez tous ces chiens près du supermarché. Je me demande où sont leurs maîtres. J'ai un chien berger° chez moi aux Etats-Unis.
Mme. Duval:	Comment votre mère supporte-t-elle un animal dans la maison? Ça, je ne voudrais pas.
Mary:	Oh, notre chien, Buster, il est adorable. Il fait partie de la famille. Il me manque beaucoup.° (Madame Duval et Mary achètent les provisions et sortent du supermarché.)
Mary:	Tenez! Encore les chiens. Où sont leurs maîtres?
Mme. Duval:	Mais, vous êtes vraiment préoccupée de ces chiens! Leurs maîtres sont peut-être en vacances comme presque tout le monde.

Why are there so many dogs in front of the supermarket?

A. The masters of those dogs are shopping. (Turn to p. 87, A)
B. Dogs are permitted to roam in France. (Turn to p. 85, B)
C. The dogs were released when the families went on vacation. (Turn to p. 87, C)
D. Many grocers in France feed roaming dogs. (Turn to p. 84, D)

---

maîtres   masters, owners   **chien berger**   German shepherd
Il me manque beaucoup.   I miss him a lot.

47. Le Réveillon

Holidays, religion

Nantes, France.

Jeanne: Dorothy, je t'invite à venir passer le réveillon chez moi.
Dorothy: Oh, c'est gentil, Jeanne. J'accepte l'invitation.
Jeanne: Nous serons une quinzaine° chez moi.
Dorothy: Quand veux-tu que je vienne chez toi?
Jeanne: Mais, tu ne sais pas ce que c'est que le réveillon? C'est une fête qui a lieu° après la messe de minuit° la veille° de Noël. C'est un grand dîner. Comme dessert on sert traditionellement la bûche° de Noël. Presque tous les Français fêtent le réveillon.
Dorothy: Tiens! Je ne savais pas qu'il y avait tant de pratiquants en France.

Are French people as pious as Dorothy seems to think?

A. Both Catholics and Protestants celebrate *le réveillon*, and most French people are rather pious. (Turn to p. 88, A)
B. It is mainly women who attend midnight mass and celebrate *le réveillon*. (Turn to p. 89, B)
C. Most French Catholics attend *le réveillon* and are therefore, rather devout in the practice of their religion. (Turn to p. 91, C)
D. Celebrating *le réveillon* does not mean that a person necessarily attends church regularly. (Turn to p. 90, D)

---

une quinzaine about fifteen
messe de minuit midnight mass
la bûche log (a cake in the shape of a log)

qui a lieu which takes place
la veille the night before

48. C'est une "Catherinette"!

Liberty, family, religion

C'est le 25 novembre. Le Havre, France.

David: J'ai lu dans *Le Figaro* qu'aujourd'hui, c'est le jour de la Sainte Catherine.

André: Oui, on fête les jeunes filles qui ont 25 ans et qui ne se sont pas mariées.

David: Que veux-tu dire?

André: Eh bien, on leur donne un bal. Elles portent des drôles de chapeaux.

David: Pourquoi est-ce qu'on les fête?

Why do the French celebrate Saint Catherine's Day?

A. To make fun of women who are not married. (Turn to p. 91, A)
B. To praise those women of 25 who have been able to resist marriage. (Turn to p. 90, B)
C. To encourage early marriages and population growth. (Turn to p. 88, C)
D. To make it easier for single men and women to meet. (Turn to p. 89, D)

49. De Grands enfants

Intellectuality, individualism

A la terrasse d'un café du Quartier Latin à Paris.

Jean: Regarde ces gens qui passent. On peut reconnaître assez facilement les étrangers, n'est-ce pas?

Hervé: Oui, d'habitude ils s'habillent d'une manière différente, et puis, ils ont souvent une allure° différente.

Jean: Regarde ces deux-là. Ce sont peut-être des Boches.° Et plus loin, ce sont des Amerloques,° sans doute.

Dick: Qu'est-ce que c'est qu'un Boche et un Amerloque?

Jean: C'est de l'argot.° Un Boche est un Allemand et un Amerloque est un Américain.

Dick: Ah oui, je vois. Donc, je suis Amerloque. (Ils rient.)

Hervé: Les Américains sont drôles. En France nous disons que ce sont "de grands enfants".

Dick: Pourquoi les Français disent-ils que les Américains sont "de grands enfants"?

Hervé: Je ne sais pas moi. Ils aiment beaucoup les sports. Ils s'amusent. Ils semblent parfois un peu naïfs.

What do the comments of Hervé and Jean indicate about their ways of thinking?

A. They know Americans rather well. (Turn to p. 98, A)
B. They respect Dick as an intelligent, well-educated young man. (Turn to p. 99, B)
C. They admire Americans. (Turn to p. 97, C)
D. They are trying to appear intellectual by generalizing all people of one nation under a label. (Turn to p. 96, D)

---

allure bearing   **Boches** (slang) negative term for Germans
Amerloques (slang) negative term for Americans
argot slang

50. Sois raisonnable!

Individualism

Sur le bateau scolaire qui va en Europe, deux étudiants français et deux étudiants américains préparent la première édition du journal du bateau. Les voilà réunis cet après-midi.

Margaret: Allons diviser le travail selon les sources des nouvelles.

Anne-Marie: Mais nous n'avons pas encore décidé si nous allons publier trois longues éditions qui sortent tous les deux jours, ou six petites éditions qui sortent tous les jours. Je crois qu'il faut en faire une tous les jours.

Pierre: Mais non, Anne-Marie, comme je t'ai déjà dit, nous n'aurons pas le temps de préparer une édition tous les jours. On veut faire quelque chose de valeur.

Anne-Marie: Mais tu ne comprends pas un des premiers principes du bon reportage, c'est qu'il faut sortir le journal avant que les nouvelles soient trop vieilles.

Ronald: Margaret et moi, nous avons déjà dit ce matin que trois éditions ou six éditions, cela nous est égal.° Et. . .

Pierre: Mais nous ne voulons pas nous dégrader dans le bas journalisme, des mondanités,° des faits divers,° qui n'intéressent personne. C'est pour ça qu'il faut s'occuper des vrais nouvelles, ce qui prend du temps. Il faut que nous sortions le journal tous les deux jours.

Anne-Marie: Pierre, tu es têtu.° Sois raisonable! Ne vois-tu pas que. . .

Pierre: Je suis raisonnable, moi, C'est toi qui n'es pas raisonnable.

Margaret: Raisonnable ou pas, si cela continue, nous ne sortirons pas du tout le journal.

Why is it taking so long to come to an agreement?

A. The two Americans have not committed themselves to one or the other of the two principles. (Turn to p. 102, A)

B. The French have difficulty agreeing with each other. (Turn to p. 101, B)

C. Pierre is stubborn. (Turn to p. 100, C)

D. Anne-Marie is stubborn. (Turn to p. 102, D)

---

les nouvelles the news   **cela nous est égal** it's all the same to us
mondanités society news   **faits divers** minor news   **têtu** stubborn

Follow-ups

A. There are probably people in every society who are somewhat intimidated by teachers, especially if their teachers have been authoritarian. Most people, however, realize that their "bad" impressions of particular teachers were established at an age when they were more mischievous and restless than they would like to admit. In any case, Franz and Diane's colleagues would not be intimidated by these two foreign teachers. Read the selection again and make another choice.

B. Most people in France would not consider Charles lazy. Reread the selection and choose another response.

C. "Coldness" is an observation based on the values of one's native culture. The manner of acting in a foreign culture should be analyzed according to the values of that culture. French people do not consider French women "cold" or unapproachable. Choose again.

D. It is unlikely that the actions of the two girls would have revealed that they were students. In any case, business people, above all, want to sell their products. They try not to alienate their clients. Try again.

A. Françoise has indeed shown frustration with the situation, but anger is not unusual here, considering the fact that the French are extremely particular about their food. The international reputation of French cooking must be upheld. Choose another answer.

B. It is true that many French people will toast a job well done, a change of rank, a new baby, a new job, etc., but Guy is not making up a reason for celebrating. By knowing that, you may have a clearer idea which choice is correct. Choose again.

C. Teachers do expect a lot of their students in France, but the *bac* exam that Hélène took was not graded by her teachers, but by impartial, carefully selected teachers. Choose another response.

D. In the conversation, Marie-Claude states that they would meet in front of the restaurant. It is not uncommon for young people to meet at a public place, convenient for all parties, before continuing on to the evening's entertainment. When a fellow begins to pick a girl up at her home, the relationship has become rather serious, for that involves the family. Choose again.

A. This is surely one of the reasons why some cars do not stop to pick up hitchhikers in Europe; they stand on the highway where it would be difficult for a car to stop without risking an accident. But the exact location of the two hitchhikers on the highway has not been mentioned. Therefore, it is not the best answer. Try again.

B. The French are usually quite tolerant of foreigners. Reread the conversation again and make another choice.

C. In France, parents and teachers often criticize slang, but what they are really criticizing is the use of slang in formal situations and in writing, where it is not appropriate. Most French parents and teachers do use slang in informal situations. Choose another answer.

D. There may be some reflection on one's ancestry if a person has recently moved up in the class structure. But, if he or she has attained both an excellent education and also a strong financial standing, his or her ancestry is unimportant, and usually unknown to others. Try again.

A. Generalizations such as "French girls do not like American men" are usually made in an effort to find a simple explanation for something one does not understand. Try again.

B. The French students do miss the native cuisine when they leave their country. There are certain American foods Americans miss when they are abroad. However, we are looking for something deeper, such as a reason for "distrusting" American food. Does that information give you a clue to the correct answer? Choose again.

C. Correct! There is a greater awareness of class differences in France than in the United States. Status and class in France are determined in large part by the amount of one's education. Even though university tuition is virtually free in France, because of low salaries, it is still a heavy burden on the lower socio-economic class families to pay the room and board expenses for a son or daughter at a lycée or a university. Some Scholarships do exist for superior lycée and university students from low-income families, but many of these young people are encouraged to work instead.

D. Taxes on automobiles are higher in France than in the United States. Owning a car is a luxury. French automobiles are smaller, but still quite expensive. Gas is also highly taxed and now costs much more than in the United States. Cars do not cost twice as much as in the United States, however. Choose again.

A. Pierre is trying to cross the border with only two boxes of cigars in excess of the number permitted; perhaps they are for his uncle who has a weakness for Cuban cigars. There is nothing said which would suggest that Pierre is a trafficker in drugs. Try another answer.

B. Correct! Although many French students have motorbikes or scooters, which use a lot less gas than automobiles, (gas is more expensive in France than in the U.S.) French parents do not usually permit their children to have cars, for a number of reasons, including the following: (1)the public transportation system is adequate and (2) French parents would not do anything which would hinder their child's attainment of a good education. Upward mobility in France is directly tied to attainment of the baccalaureate degree. In any case, the school day is much longer in France, and lycée students are usually loaded down with homework, so there is no time for a part-time job to pay for a car.

C. It is unusual in France for a girl to ask a fellow to go out with her. That information should help you find the correct answer. Choose again.

D. Correct! Although the Frenchman prides himself in being an individual, he tends to be quite conformist in matters of dress, of taste, and of etiquette or social propriety. The expression *Ça ne se fait pas*! ("It just isn't done!") indicates the unquestioning acceptance of the code. One Frenchman explained why he kept his sport coat on in the train as follows: "Even though it is very hot, the thought of taking off my sport coat never entered my mind."

A. This is possible, but it is not the right answer. We're trying to find the cultural conflict which caused the lady to become angry. Reread the conversation and choose again.

B. The use of the *tu* form and the expression *mon vieux* does indicate friendship, but a friendship no different from any other in a social group. Does that give you a hint as to the correct response? Choose again.

C. University students from middle-income families, as well as those from very rich families, usually do not work during the summer. Try again.

D. It is certain that some French people do not like Americans, just as it is certain that some Americans do not like the French. This is usually because of ignorance of each others' cultures. It would not be accurate to generalize such a feeling to an entire population, however. In this conversation the Belgian, Jean-Paul, mistakenly attributed the displaying of the American flag as the most important reason why he was not being picked up. Or, perhaps, not being American, he resented being indicated as one. Study the conversation again and make another choice.

A. An American visiting France might notice a tendency among some French people to portray foreigners according to preconceived notions. However, this stereotyping exists everywhere, because of the general ignorance people have of each other's cultures. People look for a simple explanation for *complicated* cultural phenomena. This tendency is undoubtedly more visible in France because of the French people's love for the exchange of ideas. In many French families, from the time children are very small, they are encouraged to express their opinions. The French are usually tolerant of foreigners, as long as their lives are not disturbed by them. Choose again.

B. Either candy or flowers would be appropriate. Reread the conversation and make another choice.

C. Pierre's comment that he will perhaps recover is a typical example of French irony and realism. His comment about perhaps recovering should not be taken literally. Reread the conversation and try again.

D. What one person values as "the finer things money can buy" may be totally different from what another person prizes. In this case, Charles' parents undoubtedly value highly the benefits of foreign travel for their son. Their son may do better in his English class in the fall and may do better on the baccalaureate exam. Reread the selection and choose a more appropriate response.

A.   Madame Foucart's comment *Elle est sympathique* would seem to imply that she does not dislike her, and monsieur Foucart does not express any dislike for the girl. Choose another response.

B.   Since Mary was holding up and admiring a peach, not acting suspiciously, it is unlikely the fruit seller would think the girls were attempting to shoplift. Choose again.

C.   Correct! The French are very sociable with people they know well, but they rarely invite these friends into their home. They might meet friends at a café or meet at a convenient place before going on to a movie together. The home is for the family, which often includes parents, grandparents, aunts, uncles, and cousins. For many French people, to apply the same attention to outsiders as to family members would be to diminish the closeness of the family. Foreigners are generally transitory, since they soon return to their home country. Furthermore, to invite someone to one's home is a very special occasion indeed, which takes many hours of preparation and considerable expense. Usually included are a meal with carefully prepared homemade dishes, three or four special wines, three or four cheeses, a delicious French cake or pastry for dessert, and the choice of cognac or scotch as *digestif*. Few people want to undertake such an elaborate affair for foreigners, or even friends. Finally, the French spend, on the average, considerably less on housing (much more on food and recreation) than Americans do. Therefore, the French may feel that Americans, many with their four-and five-bedroom homes, would be incapable of appreciating their more modest dwellings.

D.   Being students, the girls may have had classes to attend. However, they did not mention classes to attend, and even if they had, that would not explain the abruptness of their departure. Try again.

A. Correct! Up until very recently French Catholics had been permitted to name their babies only with a saint's name. A French person celebrates his or her date of birth, his or her saint's day, or both. Some French adults celebrate neither, as they consider such celebrations for children.

B. Correct! Although nothing in what the two boys said may seem objectionable according to American standards, forwardness and immediate use of first names does not conform to the French pattern of formality. The French are often admired for their good manners when first meeting people. This ritualistic *politesse* serves to keep the two parties at a distance until they become friends. In the conversation, the boys' excessive familiarity is evidenced by Paul's immediate use of the *tu* form; this is inappropriate between strangers. The boys were too forward, and the girls did not want to be too friendly toward total strangers.

C. Correct! The French keep a certain polite distance when conversing with a stranger; they generally do not go out of their way to meet and greet strangers. Since they would not invite a new acquaintance into their homes, it is not unusual that they would not invite a complete stranger into their automobiles with them. This would be particularly true if the driver knew that the hitchhikers were foreigners.

D. The alcoholic content of French and American wines is generally similar. In any case, becoming tipsy is determined by the lack of restraint of the person drinking, rather than by the alcoholic content of the beverage being drunk. Choose again.

A. Lycée and university students in France generally do not work to earn money in the summer and do not have the time during the school year. Choose again.

B. Correct! The French, of course, would prefer that a foreigner not "murder their language." However, they would prefer the "murdering of their language" to the silence of a visitor who would not speak for fear of making a grammatical mistake. The French love to converse and to exchange ideas. French children are often encouraged to express their ideas. This causes a lot of uninformed opinions, but to the French that is not usually as important as the delight in the exchange. Indeed, occasionally a French person will argue an idea he or she does not really believe in. Needless to say, an American should never hope or expect to get the French to agree with him or her. The French generally consider the American shallow if he or she does what we Americans have often grown up learning to do: to gain acceptance by literally being "agreeable," in the sense of agreeing with everything a particular person is saying. Betty would have been happier had she concentrated a little more on the exchange of ideas, rather than the fear of making grammatical mistakes. The Foucarts would have been pleased.

C. For any modern society to be functioning at all, there must be respect for the laws. Otherwise there is anarchy. There is less crime in France than in the United States. Choose a more appropriate response.

D. Since Harold had expressed his appreciation to the woman for having shown them to their seats, and since Harold might have smiled at her at the same time, it is unlikely that she would have been insulted. Try again.

A. Correct! Lycée and university students in France generally do not hold jobs. Students are expected to study while in school and work after completing their education. Unlike their American counterparts French secondary and university students have very few expenses: (1) students pay reduced fares on public transportation; (2) tuition is virtually nonexistent; (3) many students do not pay room and board since they live at home; (4) there are special student rates at school cafeterias, movies, plays, etc. Because of this tradition of not working until after finishing one's education, most French students are free to study, or to travel at reduced rates (living cheaply in youth hostels). Most lycée students study at least two foreign languages and traveling improves their knowledge of the languages. As more students from lower socio-economic classes are entering the lycée and the university, this tradition is beginning to break down somewhat.

B. It is doubtful that Sara would be expressing prejudices against farmers. Most French families have some ancestors who were farmers. Try again.

C. Since Betty has been so silent with the Foucarts, it would not be surprising that the Foucarts might believe Betty to be dissatisfied in some way. Madame Foucart, however, concluded that Betty is timid, not angry with them. Choose again.

D. Intelligence is relative, and there are other equally important factors in determining whether or not a student is prepared to take an exam. Choose again.

A. Correct! In France, students normally go out in groups, rather than date in couples. Everyone pays his or her own way. Two members of the group may eventually begin to go out as a couple, but they will usually continue to participate in at least some of the group activities. Some Americans who have lived in France have praised this system, claiming that it does give young people time to get to know each other before dating. In this conversation the pronoun *on* refers to an indefinite number of persons. Marie-Claude was referring to "they" and "we" in the sense of the entire group, whereas, David thought she was referring to "we two." The cultural misunderstanding was caused by David evaluating French cultural patterns according to the values and customs of his own native culture.

B. Since the two boys are traveling together, they obviously like each other and enjoy each other's company. Choose again.

C. Keeping a sport coat on will indeed protect a white shirt from getting dirty. However, French trains are not usually dirty. Search again for a better reason why the Frenchman keeps his coat on despite the heat.

D. The French enjoy discussing politics and usually do not agree with each other, almost as a matter of principle. This generally causes no deep-seated anger. Try again.

A. Some French men seem to be fearful of catching cold from a draft. There is a more appropriate reason, however. Try again.

B. In France, students and soldiers who have little money hitchhike to avoid paying railroad or bus fare. As the people in the conversation are young, they would not be considered "bums" in France. Try again.

C. The standard of living in France is not much lower than in the United States; values are different. In France, one's income corresponds more closely to one's education than in the United States. However, this is not the principal reason why most French students do not have cars. Try again.

D. Correct! Because the French believe so strongly in the principles of order and organization, they tend to make long lists of regulations. Many government officials pride themselves at interpreting these regulations to the letter. The French people have developed what they call *le système* D. or *le système* débrouillard, which can be defined as being clever enough to find a way to get through the regulations and red tape. Since virtually all modes of transportation in France are government run, as are the post office, the telephone, the telegraph, the social security system (which includes both retirement and medical care for all citizens), and a number of industries (aviation, shipbuilding, Renault, tobacco, etc.), a French person confronts government regulations daily. Cheating the government on taxes, for example, is not considered as reprehensible in France as it is in the United States. In this conversation, another French person would probably have been glad to help Pierre get around a customs regulation.

A. Correct! The baccalaureate exam is so difficult in France that only about one third of the students pass. Scores between 12 and 20 are passing. Students who receive scores between 8 and 12 may take an oral make-up exam, but must score at least 10 to pass. Those scoring below 8 may take the exam the following year. French students are generally fairly realistic and philosophical about failing these exams. They know they have two more chances to take the exam at the end of the academic year. They know they must study harder next time, but there is some consolation in the fact that more people fail than pass. However, the disappointment is nevertheless very strong, since the *bac* is required for the better positions, and is required for entrance into the university. In the conversation, Bill was applying American cultural patterns to those of the French, which is inaccurate. In the United States many more students receive high school diplomas.

B. This is possible; the woman may have realized they were Americans by their dress and accent. Even so, there was something they had done, or not done, to anger her. Choose again.

C. Even if Guy were not particularly religious, he still might celebrate his saint's day. Choose again.

D. Friendship often does grow deeper because of shared experiences over an extended period of time. However, many friendships also grow quickly, in less than a year's time. Reread the conversation and choose again.

A. For this occasion, roses were appropriate. Chrysanthemums would not have been appropriate, since they are displayed only at funerals and on Memorial Day. Flowers are generally important to the French people, as they display flowers in their homes throughout the year. Try again.

B. There is a great deal more conformity and formality of dress in France than in the United States. Appropriate dress in public does not include a great deal of originality and variation of style and color. The general tendency is to conform to acceptable standards of fashion, rather than to show off one's clothes. In France often an American can be noticed by his or her dress. Choose again.

C. Correct! *Le service n'est pas compris* means that the service the lady just rendered is not included in the price of the ticket. In France, a small tip is expected by ushers at theaters, concerts, and movie theaters. Since the establishments for which these people work pay them small wages, an usher's livlihood depends on tips.

D. Correct! Nothing is wrong. French people speak at least two levels of language, formal and informal, according to the situation. Here Françoise is speaking in an informal situation and feels free to speak in a very light and even slightly vulgar manner. Many French parents and teachers would also use such slang in a similar situation. However, if Françoise were speaking with her parents, teachers, or strangers, she would say the same thing in a more formal, polite style.

A.   Twenty years ago there were still some isolated villages in France which did not have an adequate supply of sanitary drinking water. This is no longer true. Wine to many French people is the preferred beverage. For others bottled mineral water and spring water (l'eau d'Evian, l'eau de Vichy, Perrier, etc.) are considered to be healthier than regular tap water or wine. Seeing the French drink bottled water or wine should not imply that French tap water is any less safe than American tap water. Choose again.

B.   On the contrary, the French consider themselves individualists and pride themselves in their critical spirit. To the French, being critical and analytical indicates intelligence. Some, of course, are overly critical. Emphasizing the positive, rather than the negative, is certainly not a French trait. Choose again.

C.   Correct! Madame Bertrand expected and appreciated the flowers. Her comment that Jane shouldn't have brought flowers and that she was *confuse* should not be taken literally. Social proprieties in France demand just such a reaction on the part of the host or hostess when presented with flowers. In France social proprieties, especially those surrounding the family and the home, are almost ritualistic.

D.   France has the world's highest death rate from cirrhosis of the liver, but the number of victims is a very small fraction of the entire population. The comment *J'ai mal au foie* would not mean that one has cirrhosis of the liver. That serious illness, which seems to result in part from excessive consumption of alcoholic beverages, would be expressed more in terms of *une maladie du foie*. Choose again.

A. It is unlikely that Pierre wants sympathy. Choose again.

B. Excessive drinking does, of course, exist in France. However, moderation in all things is a principle the French, in general, try to instill in their children from a very young age. The average French person, when he or she drinks, usually drinks a small amount, and seldom consumes enough to be inebriated, which is thought to be in very bad taste. Choose again.

C. Correct! Fruit sellers in France are proud of their displays which are very often arranged in geometric fashion. Many believe that fruit handled by customers could not only become bruised, but also could hinder the entire appearance of the shop. French clients realize this and act accordingly.

D. French children usually are given less freedom and more discipline than American children. The educational theory which is most pervasive in France is that children should be first restricted, trained, and educated in order that they later will be able to profit from their experiences and be able to channel their creativity into acceptable forms. In contrast, in the United States the pervasive educational theory is in favor of permitting the child to experience as many things as possible on his or her own, without a great deal of guidance and restrictions. The child is supposed to be creative and learn from all experiences. That is, of course an over-simplification, but nevertheless shows the different orientations in child-raising in the two countries. French children are generally not babied. Try again.

A. If they had taken the wrong seats, the woman would more than likely have pointed to the seats they were supposed to take. Choose again.

B. Since the French system of education is centralized and highly regulated, there is little variation in what is taught in a particular course throughout all schools in France, including those in the overseas *départements*, Martinique and Guadelupe. The quality of instruction is therefore fairly uniform throughout the country. Furthermore, the government has some control over which teachers are placed where. Therefore, the teachers in small towns are usually as well-prepared as those in the large cities. Choose again.

C. Correct! The French are generally suspicious of processed and artificially preserved foods, as well as canned and frozen foods. They respect nature and things natural; this springs in part from the close roots the French people have to the soil. It also comes from their analytical, independent spirit which causes them to be reluctant to try new products simply because they are new. What's more, the discovery over the past decade of a number of cancer-producing agents in certain processed and preserved foods has been reported in the French as well as in the American press.

D. Jane had not been misinformed; it is appropriate to bring flowers or candy when invited to dinner in France. Choose again.

A. American food, as a matter of fact, has a bad reputation in France. In the July 1976 issue of *Le Point* the results of a highly-respected poll indicated that the average French person believes that the most undesirable aspect about America is the quality of food Americans eat. But we are looking for the answer to why American food has a bad reputation, not whether or not, or to what degree, it is considered undesirable. Does that give you a clue to the correct answer? Choose again.

B. Correct! French people often use the term *mal au foie* when they are suffering from indigestion.

C. Correct! Note that Jake and Patty arrived in Tours on the 14th of July, French Independence Day. This holiday is celebrated with great excitement, and often with considerable overindulgence in alcoholic beverages. Most French people, however, may drink heavily only once or twice a year during very special occasions such as Independence Day. There is a *joie de vivre* in the French character which causes a person to drink for joy rather than for dispair: to congratulate someone for a job well done, to show a gesture of friendship, or to pay for a small service or favor rendered.

D. It is possible that Guy would like a party. However, to apply a generalization of that sort to an entire people is very risky, unless one has substantial information to back up the argument. Choose again.

A. Correct! Physical demonstrations involving touching, kissing, and embracing are much more common in France than in the United States. Even outside of the family, two men who are very good friends may hug each other. This of course, is also true as far as two women friends are concerned. The daily handshake is, of course, obligatory when meeting acquaintances, friends, and co-workers.

B. The father's driving is an example of letting one's emotions affect one's judgement and one's ability to drive prudently. It is very probable that the father does *know how* to drive well. It would be an exaggeration to say that most French people act just as foolishly when driving as the father in this conversation. Choose again.

C. Correct! A French person who loses his or her place in line has not defended it. Occasionally some one will try to get in at the head of a line, and the others must defend their places.

D. Correct! The *surveillants* are not teachers, but university students. By not having to do such things as hall duty and cafeteria duty, the French teacher is able to devote more time to his or her academic duties. This reflects the high respect accorded to teachers in France.

A. Jokes are usually played on people one knows, not on strangers. Purposefully leading a foreigner astray would not be considered a joke. Choose again.

B. Since Françoise said "What's extraordinary about that?", the implication in her statement is that she had indeed seen the men embracing. Choose again.

C. Correct! Many of the smaller hotels in France and other European countries have community showers in the hallway. The more luxurious hotels may have a private shower in each room. Of course, the price for such rooms is then considerably higher. Since many Europeans do not shower daily, they consider a community shower sufficient.

D. Correct! Arnold mistakenly applied American dating habits to the French. Young people in France usually go out in groups of friends, and the group usually is not composed of an equal number of boys and girls. Therefore, for one person to pay the bill for everyone would be unrealistic. Since most students do not have jobs and have very little money, the tradition is for each one to pay his or her own share.

A. Mr. Wenstrom understood correctly when the management told him that the hotel had showers. What he did not know was that the showers would be at the end of the hallways, not in the rooms. The management therefore, did not lie to Mr. Wenstrom. Choose again.

B. Correct! The first floor on ground floor in the United States is called *rez de chaussée* in France. Therefore, in France *le premier étage* is indeed the second floor of American buildings.

C. Arnold thought that Jacqueline was ungrateful because she did not let him pay her way. He was, however, making the mistake of applying American dating habits to French people. Choose again.

D. It is always possible to mistake the number of floors one has climbed, especially if one has climbed several floors. Paul seems very sure of the number he has climbed, however. Choose again.

A. Dating in America has its unspoken rules and regulations, one of which is that the fellow should usually pay the girl's expenses. In France young people usually go out in groups. The main considerations are friendship and having a good time, and sometimes the group will be composed of three boys and five girls, or three girls and five boys, or any other ratio. Even when a boy and a girl begin to feel romantically inclined, they still go out often in the group with their friends. Choose again.

B. The Wenstroms' first reaction to the room was very positive, and this mini-drama does not indicate how nice the other rooms in the hotel were in comparison with the one the Wenstroms were given. Therefore, we could not conclude that that room was worse than others. Choose again.

C. The tobacconist, like any merchant, does not want to alienate a possible customer. The tobacconist laughed, since he was just as convinced that the tourist bureau was on the *deuxième étage* as Paul was convinced that it was on the "third floor." Choose again.

D. Because of the variety of conceptions of morality and the difficulty of always being able to define what is universally moral, it is a hasty generalization to suggest that one entire population is more moral than another. Choose again.

A. Since families are very close in France, the average parents are very careful in the raising of their children. Serving wine in moderation, just as other foods are served, keeps children from seeing wine as a forbidden, desirable drink. Try again.

B. The French enjoy the outdoor cafés very much and do frequent them regularly, as do most foreigners who come to visit France. In the month of August when most Parisians leave the city to go on vacation, it is very possible that most of the people in the cafés would be foreigners. However, we have not been told that this conversation has taken place in the month of August. Choose again.

C. French students, on the contrary, generally do respect their teachers, since they know that it is only by succeeding at school that they will get good jobs. Consequently, students are under a great deal of pressure from their parents to do well in school. French teachers usually have a good command of the subject they teach. Choose again.

D. Anne only expressed distaste for the relative cleanliness, or dirtiness, of the streets of Boston. She did not mention any other aspects about Boston. We do not have enough information to conclude that Anne likes or dislikes Boston. Try again.

A. Mrs. White jumped to a conclusion when she suggested that French people sitting in outdoor cafés were wasting their time. The accurate way of determining how hard-working people are is to watch them in their work, not in their periods of relaxation. Choose again.

B. There is no indication that it is not wine that the children are drinking. When the family has dinner in a restaurant, wine is an appropriate drink. Choose again.

C. Americans are often sensitive about criticism of their country, even though the criticism may be merited. However, we have no reason to believe that this is the case here. It is just as possible that Johnny sincerely believes that Boston is clean. Choose again.

D. Madame Levallois actually did not try to quiet the students. They became quiet on their own. Try again.

A. It is possible that a foreigner may be sensitive about criticism of his or her country. However, we have no reason to believe that that is the case here. It is possible that Anne sincerely believes that Paris is clean. Choose again.

B. It would be an oversimplification to say that American teachers are stronger disciplinarians. Generally, a great deal more is permitted of American students before they are considered "out of line." Choose again.

C. Correct! The French pride themselves in what they call *savoir vivre*, the right balance between work and play. The ability to keep their perspective, the ability to not become overly involved in work, and the ability to enjoy and appreciate life are all important to the French. Many French people see the Americans as never having attained that balance.

D. Correct! The French believe that it is wise psychologically to serve a little wine to children as they grow up. The children then see wine as simply another beverage, without the mystery and attraction it would have if it were forbidden. Usually only one small glass is permitted children, and usually that glass is half water and half wine.

A. Correct! Many American teachers will not begin a class until all students are quiet. The students usually realize that and quiet down when they see the teacher is ready to start. In contrast, many French teachers will begin talking before the students have quieted down. The students realize this and stop talking when they hear the professor starting the class. As for *le chahut*, the sudden burst of noise, the students had reacted to something the teacher had said. Since they became calm immediately afterward, they must have respected her. A better sign of a lack of class discipline is continuous noise.

B. Correct! Cleanliness is variable from society to society. What one society considers to be clean, another society may consider to be dirty. Such is the case here. Streets in France are usually kept extraordinarily clean according to American standards; street cleaners wash down the streets, sweep them in places, and pick up paper. In America, it is not always noticed if the streets are "a little dirty." Some Americans, used to new modern facades of buildings, would consider the dark facades of many French buildings as dirty. The French seldom, if ever, notice the relative cleanliness or dirtiness, of the facades of their buildings. This variability of cleanliness exists in many other areas of daily living.

C. A view of morality which includes only consideration of the drinking of a beverage is indeed a very narrow view of morality. Choose again.

D. Many business dealings have been carried out in outdoor cafés in France. Many students and writers often do their work in cafés. However, this is not the right answer. Try again.

A. Joyce seems to think that a *surveillant* is a teacher on hall duty, since in the United States some teachers are given hall and cafeteria duties. In France the teachers do not perform these tasks. Joyce misunderstood Mr. Renard. Try again.

B. A French person might pay the bill for everyone and then expect the other person or persons to pay the bill the next time. That is not so, however, with students. Does that clue help you find the correct answer? Choose again.

C. If Françoise were acting blasé and worldly, that would mean that she had been just as astonished as the American boys. However she is from a different culture and will therefore often react differently. Her comment: "What is unusual?" should be taken at face value. Choose again.

D. Although it is true that homes in the United States have more bathtubs and showers than those in France, it is also true that there are many more homes in France with a bidet than in the U.S. It would be inaccurate, therefore, to draw conclusions about the relative degrees of cleanliness of the French and the American from this information. Choose again.

A. Correct! Although most French people are not as foolhardy as the father in this conversation, many do seem to act as if their cars are an extension of themselves. Cursing each other is prevalent among French drivers. This is one of the important reasons why some French people prefer to travel by train when going on vacation, even when they have a car.

B. It is possible that a line crasher might make up such a story in order to try to get a better place in line. The man did not get excited for that reason, however, since he did not know for sure if the woman was actually the line crasher's wife. Choose again.

C. Although this *surveillant* happens to be stationed in the recreation area where some of the physical education courses are given, he is not a physical education instructor. Choose again.

D. According to American cultural phenomenon, a logical possible explanation might be that the children had recently been punished and were therefore quieter than usual. However, no punishment has been mentioned. Since we are studying French children in their French cultural context, we must look for *French* reasons for their behavior. Try again.

A. To the foreigner who does not know why the people of a particular country act a certain way, the first reaction is to attribute those actions to irrational behavior. There is usually a reasonable explanation why foreigners get excited. Try again.

B. Although the *surveillant* is usually younger than the teachers, he is not one of the older lycée students. Try again.

C. French children are permitted to speak at the table, but in moderation. Does that information help you find the correct answer? Try again.

D. There are many two-lane highways in France. It is, of course, dangerous to pass on the two-lane highways, especially when there is a lot of traffic. This is not, however, the best answer. Choose again.

A.   Correct! Since there is a great deal of closeness in the French family, and since French children are used to minding their parents, those children are not the little martyrs that they may seem to be to an American like Joe. In contrast, American children are often encouraged to talk and are given a great deal of attention at the table. Just as Joe misinterpreted the relationship the Petit children had with their parents, it is common for French people to misinterpret the greater freedom of American children as a complete lack of respect for their parents.

B.   From the American point of view it may appear that the father is a tyrant. However, Mr. Petit is a Frenchman. His actions must be analyzed and interpreted in the context of his own culture. Choose again.

C.   Putting other people's lives in danger could hardly be considered as "having fun." Try again.

D.   According to American standards, the man would perhaps be considered ill-tempered. However, the man is French and is acting according to French cultural values which must be considered. Try again.

A. According to American culture, it is appropriate for strangers to notice little children or babies in public. The parents appreciate the attention and consider it a tribute to themselves as well as to their children. But this situation is taking place in France, which has its own value system. Choose again.

B. This answer is partly true. However, they have a more important reason for putting trees, shrubbery, walls, and fences around homes. Choose again.

C. It is very possible that Hélène does appreciate what the Browns have done for her. Being sensitive to the Browns' feelings, however, is something else. Try again.

D. It is possible that a few grocers might take pity on the starving dogs, but it is more likely that the dogs are attracted by the smell of meat in the butcher shops. Choose again.

A. Correct! This may be the greatest source of conflict between the Americans and the French. In conversation the average American often tries to find a basis upon which to agree in order to have a harmonious, pleasant conversation. Usually this basis is established before more serious ideas are exchanged. When one person does not agree with the other, he or she tries to soften the disagreement rather than emphasize it. In contrast, the French person loves to debate, even to the point of making provocative comments. The basis of American conversation is diametrically opposed to the French. Consequently, the American should learn to be a little less sensitive and realize that the French person does not necessarily dislike him or her. In order to better understand and relate to the French, an American could be a little less cautious in conversation. He or she should be ready to debate, and ready to have fun while doing so. In this conversation, Hélène was merely stating the fact that the French prefer houses made of brick and stone rather than wood. She meant no .harm.

B. No. Dogs are not permitted to roam in France. It is not only unusual but unlawful that these dogs are not being cared for by their owners. Choose again.

C. Correct! It is an American tradition to pay attention to little babies and children and to express how beautiful they are. This compliment is directed to the children, but perhaps is intended more for the parents. This manner of getting immediately involved with total strangers is contrary to the French character.

D. The sliding iron grates placed in front of some store doors and windows are to keep out criminals. But this protective function of barriers in front of stores should not be confused with the function of barriers placed around private homes. Try again.

A. Correct! The importance of privacy is reflected in the isolation the French try to achieve by placing walls, fences, bushes, and trees around their homes. The French visiting the United States are surprised to see how many American homes are often void of surrounding shrubs and trees.

B. The easy way of reacting to complicated cultural phenomenon is to draw a generalization from *one* person or *one* experience in a foreign culture and apply it to *all* people and *all* situations in that culture. That, of course, is inaccurate and leads to prejudice. Perhaps most Americans and many French people would consider Hélène rather insensitive in this situation. Certainly it would be hasty to conclude that all French people are insensitive. Choose again.

C. The French are not required by law to build walls. There are many French homes without walls at all, but with many trees and shrubs instead. Try again.

D. In some American circles, a person who does not notice babies and little children is thought to dislike them. This is not so in France. Even if the French do not make a fuss over children, it should not be said that they do not appreciate children. Try again.

A. It is quite likely that, if the masters of those dogs had been shopping, they would have already left with their dogs by the time Madame Duval and Mary had finished their shopping. Try again.

B. Most little American children would smile back and appreciate the attention. But, here we are studying the reactions of a French child, who, in these circumstances, would not be considered too serious if he did not smile. Choose again.

C. Correct! Americans are rather unique among people in the extent that they love animals and pets. There are some parts of the world where animals we traditionally consider as pets are raised as food: horses, dogs, cats. Some Americans seem to adore their animals as much as other members of the family. Only in America are there pet cemeteries. French people, in general, do not care for pets as much as Americans do. Recently more French people have been acquiring pets. When the people go on vacation in the month of August, there are not enough kennels available for all dogs. They cannot ask a friend to take care of their dog since their friend is most likely on vacation also. That is why many French people release their pets when they go on vacation in the month of August. The French Society for the Prevention of Cruelty to Animals has been speaking out strongly against this practice.

D. Obviously there has been some misunderstanding, since the Browns have reacted rather strongly. As with other conflicts with foreign people, it is best to try to find the reason why Hélène acted as she did, rather than concluding so hastily that she dislikes the Browns. It is also very possible that she likes the Browns very much. Choose again.

A.   The tradition of *le réveillon*, or dinner after the midnight services, exists for both Protestants and Catholics. However, many people celebrate *le réveillon* without first going to the midnight church services, and still others may attend the midnight church services, but not attend church throughout the rest of the year. Choose again.

B.   Amy wants to profit from a foreign trip and is, therefore, probably not lazy. She seems impressed by the amount of time French students devote to school classes and homework. That does not necessarily mean she is lazy. Choose again.

C.   The object of the celebration is not to encourage marriage. Choose again.

D.   James could have been exposed to the music of French poet-singers in the United States. He would not have needed to go to France to be exposed to such songs. Choose again.

A. The school day is long in France. For many American students the school day is long also; they remain at school after classes in order to participate in sports, music, drama, and other exta-curricular activities. The length of time students are at school is not why Amy considers student life so serious in France. Try again.

B. Traditionally, women and children have attended church more regularly than men in France. However, this trend seems to be breaking down. In any case, attendance at the midnight mass is not necessary for attendance at the *réveillon*. Both men and women attend *le réveillon* which is really just a late, elaborate, Christmas dinner celebration. Choose again.

C. French pop music is fairly similar to American popular music. Even if James had heard French popular music, he still would be unaware of the type of music Anne is referring to. Try again.

D. One of the side benefits of the Saint Catherine Day parties is that there is a lot of humorous matchmaking. However, since Saint Catherine's Day only happens once a year, it is certainly not very useful for introducing men and women to each other. Choose again.

A. Correct! The fact that several poet-singers have remained popular in France over a period of years illustrates the French interest in poetry and the intellectual. George Brassens, for example, receives considerable praise for the content of his songs. The closest phenomenon in America to these poet-singers was perhaps the late Carl Sandburg, who sang some of his poems. Another example of this type of music is seen in the works of Jacques Brel. The uniqueness of Jacques Brel's songs was presented to the American public several years ago in a Broadway musical entitled "Jacques Brel is Alive and Well and Living in Paris." The French poet-singers set poetry to music.

B. Correct! Young people in France are very careful about getting married. They are not overly idealistic concerning marriage. They seem to realize that marriage will change their lives considerably and that their desires to travel, to pursue different career options, and to develop through varied experiences may never be fulfilled once they are married. The average attitude toward the "Catherinette" is therefore one of admiration. French young people tend to marry later and have fewer divorces than their American counterparts.

C. Many of the French are critical of American schools because they do not have a baccalaureate exam and because they do have a lot of sports and extra-curricular activities. For these reasons it is very possible that a French student would exaggerate the seriousness of French students in order to emphasize the contrast between what he or she believes to be the laxness of the American system and the seriousness of the French system. However, Etienne does not appear to be exaggerating the amount of homework of the average French student. Choose again.

D. Correct! Although most French people are baptized Catholics, marry in a Catholic ceremony, and are given a Catholic funeral, the average French person does not seem to believe in the dogma of the Church, or at least does not seem to think about it. The French traits of individualism, liberty, and intellectuality seem to contribute to a scepticism in matters of religion, among others. However, the French seem to feel that church is worthwhile for others, particularly for women and children. Therefore, a French person celebrating *le réveillon*, and even attending the midnight mass December 24, does not mean that he or she necessarily attends church regularly.

A.   The party is not planned to make fun of women. Choose again.

B.   James may only like love songs, but this does not explain his inability to understand the type of songs Anne is referring to. Try again.

C.   The attendance at the *réveillon* does not necessarily indicate devoutness for either Catholics and Protestants. Choose again.

D.   Correct! To the American student, used to the many school clubs, sports, dances, assemblies, etc., the French lycée, devoted strictly to the advancement of learning, appears dull and colorless. There is a tradition in American education that believes that students learn a great deal about life and human relations by participating in extra-curricular activities. This emphasis contrasts with the French emphasis on philosophy as preparation for life.

A. Correct! What the French call *football* is what we call soccer. In a sense, *football* is a more appropriate term for soccer, since soccer is played totally with the feet, never the hands. The foot is used very seldom in the playing of American football. Since the French rarely play American football, the conflict of terms only occurs when discussing sports with an American. To distinguish the two, the French use the terms *football américain* and *football français*.

B. The meat at the store where Michael shops is not necessarily of an inferior quality; it is a different kind of meat, which is in less demand. Try again.

C. Correct! In general, the French family spends a great deal more time together than does the average American family. Dinner, for instance, is a family affair which lasts sometimes for two hours or more. It is a time for talking about what happened during the day. The parents expect their children to be home in the evening preparing their homework for the following day. Teenagers seldom are permitted out in the evening on school nights. The French do not organize and join clubs to the extent the Americans do. Families often attend some recreational activities together. Since the two girls were used to that type of family life, they concluded that American family members do not have strong affections for each other.

D. It was not mispronunciation that Pierre was laughing at; he was laughing at Jerry's conception of Jean-Marie Devreux. That information should help you find the correct answer. Choose again.

A. Since in France the norm is not to be very active socially, these French girls were astonished at the Americans' many activities. They were not jealous. Choose again.

B. Correct! In French-speaking countries the tradition has been to choose names for children from saints' names. Marie is often used as a boy's second name, as in Jean-Marie Devreux. For an American, the name Jean-Marie is doubly confusing, since "Jean" and "Marie" are both girls' names in English.

C. Didier obviously knows basketball since he thought that Peter was confusing football with basketball. Choose again.

D. Correct! Most French people prefer beef to horsemeat, but horsemeat is sold throughout France. It may appear that more people in France eat horsemeat than really do because of the very noticeable statues of the horse head attached to the front of each horsemeat shop.

A. The particular type of butcher shop to which Michael is referring is often located in less affluent neighborhoods, but that is not the reason why the meat there is cheaper than in other butcher shops. Does this information give you a hint as to the correct response? Choose again.

B. It is very possible that the girls have felt that they were not getting very much attention. However, they are not spiteful toward those in their American families, since they consider them to be *sympathiques*. Rather, they are trying to analyze the consequences of American families not spending much time together. Choose again.

C. If the letter had been from two people by the names of Jean and Marie, the letter would have indicated *Jean et Marie Devreux* instead of Jean-Marie Devreux. Choose again.

D. Since the sentence "Let's play some catch" was the only English spoken, and since Peter clearly explained its meaning, Didier's command of English is not the problem here. Choose again.

A. Pierre was laughing at Jerry's conception of Jean-Marie Devreux. Does that information give you a clue to the correct answer? Choose again.

B. Didier seems convinced that he does know how to play football, as he describes confidently how to play it. The fact that he does not describe football as Peter knows it is a clue to the reason for this linguistic conflict. Choose again.

C. The horse-head butcher shops are not necessarily a chain. There is another reason why they are able to sell their meat at lower prices. Try again.

D. It is possible that the two French girls are homesick for their families, but they seem to be trying to understand the American family at this moment. Choose again.

A. In America, only educational channels are without many advertisements. In comparison, the other television channels do devote considerable time to advertisements. Choose again.

B. Although the French criticize America quite freely, they also criticize just about everything else, including themselves. Because of this critical spirit, they would not be feeling sorry for Harvey simply because he is an American. They would probably expect that he would be as proud to be an American as they are proud to be French. Choose again.

C. As Ronald implied, if one looks at the program listings, one can usually find appealing programs according to one's interests. However, most are not of high educational value. Choose again.

D. Correct! The intellectual aspect of the French character is indeed admirable. However, as in all societies, it seems that a positive trait is often misguided because of pride, fear, dishonesty, and other negative characteristics of the human species. Generalizing national groups (among other things) according to a particular catch phrase is a type of mental laziness which certainly must occur everywhere in the world. It, of course, breeds prejudice. Although it would be inaccurate to say that the French generalize more in this manner than others, such generalizations seem to be more evident in France than in many other societies (1) because of the intellectual trait in the French character and (2) because France is a tourist center and European crossroads, and therefore sees many foreigners and comments on all of them.

A. Correct! The French love to talk and to debate. This can be a positive trait or it can be a negative trait, as in this situation where these young French people are lacking in sensitivity and seem to attack the American. However, these French people do not have any personal hatred for America and Americans. They are simply accomplishing an intellectual exercise, trying to outdo each other in the display of their intellectual prowess. Obviously, they were disappointed that "America" gave up in defeat without a fight. Many Americans tend to take personally attacks on any aspect of their country. Harvey could have won respect by saying anything that appeared intelligent. This would not have been difficult, considering the rather unintelligent exaggerations and inaccuracies in the statements the French students made. They then would have respected Harvey and more than likely learned something about America in the process.

B. The American couple was not in a hurry. The mistake was failing to do something before they left. Does that hint help you find the correct answer? Choose again.

C. It is possible that they admire American achievements they might have read about or seen on television, or they may feel rather indifferent toward Americans. However, they are repeating negative names and expressions for Americans which gives the impression of a lack of respect for Americans. It is worth repeating, however, that many French people turn a critical eye toward everything, including their own society. Choose again.

D. Very rarely are advertisements placed at the beginning or the end of U.S. programs. Choose again.

A. They may be able to recognize the physical appearance of Americans and repeat the catch phrase *de grands enfants*, but that does not indicate more than a very superficial knowledge of Americans, even if that. Choose again.

B. Correct! Since Claude insisted that there were always advertisements on television, and since he never found the educational-type programs he was looking for, obviously he never found the educational television channels. Television in France is state-controlled and operated. There are virtually no advertisements. That is why Claude was so surprised to find so many advertisements on American television.

C. The French are critical of all countries, including their own. They do not think that America is particularly bad simply because they criticize it. Therefore, they would not expect Harvey to be ashamed of his country any more than they are of their own. Choose again.

D. If everybody felt that he or she should be one of the last to leave, then parties simply would not break up until very late. Choose again.

A. They obviously had been nice since both women agreed that the Americans had been *sympathiques*. Choose again.

B. The fact that the French boys would use the term *Amerloque* in front of Dick indicates that they did not expect him to understand everything they said in French nor be curious enough to ask what those words meant. Of course, he fooled them. Choose again.

C. Correct! Shaking hands with all eight persons in attendance might seem excessively formal for Americans. In France it is considered proper etiquette.

D. Harvey expressed dissatisfaction with America, which is hardly the reaction of an American captialist. Choose again.

A. Jacqueline is actually not talking about class structure. Choose again.

B. They were not talking about class structure in society. Choose again.

C. Anne-Marie accused Pierre of being stubborn. Yet she has remained as unchanged and unwilling to compromise as Pierre. Choose again.

D. It is certainly within the realm of possibility that Jean-Paul would need more practice. However, there has been no mention of his ability, or lack of ability. Choose again.

A. You cannot draw this conclusion from the facts given. Choose again.

B. Correct! Individuality is a trait of most French people. However, because of the emphasis placed upon this trait, the French are often unwilling to compromise and come to an agreement. Each one seems to believe that there is only *one* right way to do something. Since French students have seldom had the experience of working together in activities, they may not have learned that a spirit of compromise is essential for a group to achieve its goals.

C. Correct! The government prepares the driver's examinations in France. They are so rigorous that it is quite common for French people to fail the tests three or four times.

D. They were not talking about class structure. Choose again.

A. The two Americans have not contributed to Anne-Marie's and Pierre's differences of opinion. They have tried to compromise in order to get down to work and get the job done. Choose again.

B. Driving schools in France only teach. The examiners are on government salary. Choose again.

C. Correct! *Bourgeois* can mean (1) a person from the middle class or (2) a person who has the most undesirable qualities of *la bourgeoisie*, such as letting money matters take precedence over human matters or acting overly elegant or aristocratic by exaggerating speech, dress, or manners. Ellen thought that Jacqueline was referring to Françoise as in definition number one above, when actually she was referring to Françoise as in definition two.

D. Pierre and Anne-Marie call each other stubborn, yet both of them are unwilling to compromise. Choose again.

Vocabulary

The French-English vocabulary presented here represents the vocabulary as it is used in the context of this book. Cognates of identical spelling are not included. The gender of nouns is indicated by (m) and (f). Verbs are given in their infinitive forms. If a verb is reflexive, (se) follows the verb. Adjectives are listed in the masculine form with the corresponding feminine form indicated in parentheses.

A

à to, at, in
a propos de speaking of
abord: (d'abord) first
absolument absolutely
accélérer to accelerate
accompagner to accompany
achat (m) a purchase
acheter to buy
actuellement at the present time
admirer to admire
âgé (e) old
agir (s') de to be a question of
aider to help
aimablement agreeably
aimer to like, to love
aliment (m) food
allure (f) bearing, gait
allées (f pl) the goings
les allées et les venues the comings and goings
allemand(e) German
aller to go
alors then
américain(e) American

amerloque *(slang)* American
amour (m) love
amusant(e) amusing
amuser (s') to have fun
an (m) year
anglais(e) English
Angleterre (f) England
anniversaire (m) birthday
août August
appeler to call
s'appeler to be called, named
appétit (m) appetite
apporter to bring
apprécier to appreciate
apprendre to learn
après after
d'après according to
après-midi (m) afternoon
arbre (m) tree
arbuste (m) bush
argent (m) money
argot (m) slang
arrêter (s') to stop
arriver to arrive; to happen
assez enough; rather

attendre to wait for
attention attention
  faire attention to watch out
attirer to attract
aucun(e) none at all
aussi also; as
aussitôt immediately
autant as many
automobiliste (m) driver
auto-stop (m) hitchhiking
autre other
autrement otherwise
avant before
avec with
avoir to have
avril April
avouer to admit

B

baigner to bathe
  se baigner to go swimming
bal (m) party
ballon (m) ball
banlieue (f) suburbs
barrière (f) barrier
bas low
  en bas down below
bateau (m) ship, boat
beaucoup many
belge Belgian
belle beautiful, nice-looking
bête *(slang)* stupid
bien well; very
  bien sur certainly
billet (m) ticket
bizarre strange, bizarre
boche *(slang)* German
boeuf (m) beef
boire to drink
boîte (f) box
  boîte de conserve can
bon (ne) good
bondé(e) overflowing
bord (m) side
bouché(e) congested
boucherie (f) butcher shop
bouger to move
bouleversé(e) shook up
bousculer to bump against
bout (m) end
bricoler to putter

brique (f) brick
bruit (m) noise
bûche (f) log
bureau (m) office
  bureau de tourisme tourist bureau
but (m) goal

C

ça that
café (m) cafe
camarade (m,f) friend
carton (m) cardboard box
Catherinette (f) on Saint Catherine's Day, a 25 year old unmarried girl
ce this, that
cela that
célébrer to celebrate
cet this, that
cette this, that
ceux (m) these, those
chacun(e) each one
chahut (m) ruckus, uproar
chahuter to make a ruckus
chaîne (f) channel
chambre (f) room
chanter to sing
chanteur(-euse) singer
chapeau (m) hat
chaque each
chaud(e) hot
cher (chère) expensive
cheval (m) horse
chez at the place or home of
chien (m) dog
  chien berger German shepherd
chimie (f) chemistry
chimique chemical
chose (f) thing
ciao good-bye
cigarre (f) cigar
cinéma (m) movie theater
classe (f) class
club (m) club
cochonnerie *(slang)* trashy stuff
colère (f) anger
coller *(slang)* to fail
combien how much
comme as, since
commencement (m) beginning
commencer to begin
comment how, what

compartiment (m) compartment
comprendre to understand
compris included
conduire to drive
confisquer to confiscate
confus(e) embarassed
connaissance (f) acquaintance
connaître to know
consacrer to devote
conseiller(-ere) counselor
conserver to preserve
construite(e) constructed
content(e) happy
coq au vin (m) chicken cooked in wine
corne (m) horn
correspondant(e) correspondent, pen-pal
côté (à) next
couloir (m) hallway
cour (f) court
courir to run
cours (m) course
couple (m) a married couple
craigner to fear
crier to shout
croire to believe
cuisine (f) cooking
curieux(-euse) unusual; curious

D

dangereux(-euse) dangerous
dans in
de of, from
débarrasser (se) de to get rid of
débrouillarde(e) (m,f) clever person
déguelasse disgusting
déjà already
déjeuner (m) lunch
  petit déjeuner breakfast
demander to ask (for)
demi(e) half
depuis since
derrière behind
descendre to descend, go down
dessert (m) dessert
détruire to destroy
deux two
deuxième second
devant in front of
devenir to become
devoir (m) homework
devoir to have to, must
dieu God

difficile difficult
dîner to have dinner
dîner (m) dinner
dire to say, to tell
diviser to divide
dix ten
dix-huit eighteen
donc then
donner to give
dont of whom
douane (f) customs
doubler to pass (in auto)
douche (f) shower
doute (f) doubt
drapeau (m) flag
droit (m) right
drôle funny; strange
durer to last

E

échouer to fail
école (f) school
écrire to write
éducatif(-ive) educational
égal(e) equal
élève(e) high
élu(e) elected
embrasser (s') to kiss; to embrace
émigrer to immigrate
empêcher to prevent
en to, into, in; some; of it,
  of them
encore yet, still
enchanté(e) enchanted, delighted
énerver (s') to become angry or upset
enfant (m,f) child
enfin finally
enlever to take off
ennuyer to bore
  s'ennuyer to be bored
ensemble together
ensuite next, then
entendre to hear; to understand
entier(-ière) entire
entrée (f) the entrance
entrer to enter
  entrer dans la nature (slang) to go
  off the road
envers toward
envoyer to send
équipe (f) team

E continued

espérer to hope
essayer to try
étage (m) floor
Etats-Unis (m pl) United States
été (m) summer
étonner to astonish
étranger(-ere) (m, f) foreigner
être to be
étude (f) a study
étudiant(e) (m, f) student
étudier to study
évidemment evidently
examen (m) exam

F

face (f) front
  en face de opposite
fâcher (se) to become angry
facilement easily
faillir to narrowly miss
faire to do, to make
fait (m) fact
  fait diver minor news item
falloir to be necessary
famille (f) family
faute (f) fault
femme (f) woman, wife
fermier(-ière) (m, f) farmer
fête (f) celebration
fêter to celebrate
fille girl
finir to finish
fleur (f) flower
foie (m) liver
fois (f) time
  une fois once
formidable! tremendous! great!
fort(e) strong
fou (folle) crazy
frais(-aiche) fresh;cool
français(e) French
frère (m) brother
frontière (f) border
fruit (m) fruit

G

gâcher to spoil
garçon (m) boy;waiter

gare (f) station
gars (slang) guy
gêner to bother
gené(e) embarrassed
gens (m pl) people
gentil(le) nice
geste (m) gesture
gosse (slang) kid
goût (m) taste
goutte (f) drop
grand(e) big
grave serious
grilles (f pl) iron bars
  grilles d'entree entrance gate
gros(se) big; fat
guère (ne) scarcely, hardly
guerre (f) war
  La Grande Guerre First World War
guichet (m) ticket window

H

habiter to live
habitude (f) habit
  d'habitude usually
habituer (s') à to become accustomed to
hamburger (m) hamburger
heure (f) time
heureux(-euse) happy
hier yesterday
hollondais(e) Dutch
homme (m) man
honte (f) shame
hôtesse (f) hostess

I

ici here
idée (f) idea
il he; it
  il y a there is, there are
indiquer to indicate
ingrat(e) ungrateful
intéressant(e) interesting
intéresser to interest
irriter to irritate
ivrogne (m) drunkard

J

jeune young
  jeune fille (f) girl

jouer to play
jour (m) day
journal (m) newspaper
juillet July
juin June

K

klaxonner to honk

L

la the; it
là there
là-bas over there
laid(e) ugly
laisser to let, to permit
lancer to throw
langage (m) language
laver to wash
le the; it
leçon (f) lesson
légume (m) vegetable
lentement slowly
lequel which one; which
les the, them
lettre (f) letter
leur their
libre free
lieu (m) place
  avoir lieu to take place
lire to read
litre (m) liter
longtemps long, a long time
lui he; to him; her; to her
lycée (m) secondary school

M

manger to eat
manière (f) manner
main (f) hand
maintenant now
mais but
maison (f) house, home
maître (m) master
mal (m) ache, hurt
malade sick
malheureusement unfortunately
manquer to lack, to miss
manteau (m) coat
marchand(e) (m, f) merchant, clerk
marché (m) market
  bon marché inexpensive

mari (m) husband
marié(e) married
me me, to me
même same; self
mentalité (f) mentality, way of thinking
mentir to lie
mes my
messe (f) mass
mettre to put, to place
  se mettre à to begin to
mien(ne) mine
mieux better
milieu (m) middle
milliers (m pl) thousands
minuit midnight
moi me
moins less
  au moins at least
mois (m) month
mondanités (f pl) society news
monde (m) world
  tout le monde everyone
moquer (se) de to make fun of
mur (m) wall
musique (f) music

N

naïf(-ïve) naive
nécessairement necessarily
Noël Christmas
notre our
nouvelles (f pl) news
nuit (f) night

O

occuper (s') de to be busied with
offrir to give
on one, they, we
origine (f) origin
où where
ouvrir to open

P

pain (m) bread
pair (au) working for room, board, and a
  little spending money
papier (m) paper
paquet (m) package
par by

P continued

paraître to appear, to seem
parent (m, f) parent, relative
parfois at times
parler to speak
  tu parles! that's for sure!
parmi among
part (f) share
partager to share
partir to leave
passer to pass; to spend
pauvre poor
payer to pay for
paysan(ne) (m, f) peasant
peindre to paint
pendant during
  pendant que while
penser to think
perdre to lose
père (m) father
permis (m) permit
personne (ne) no one
perte (f) loss
petit(e) little
pétrole (m) oil
peu little
peur (f) fear
peut-être perhaps
phrase (f) sentence
pièce (f) play
pierre (f) stone
place (f) seat
plaire to please
plaisanter to joke
plat (m) dish
pleurer to cry
plupart (f) majority
plus more
plusieurs several
poche (f) pocket
polluer to pollute
Pologne (f) Poland
populaire popular
porte (f) door
porter to carry
pot (m) a drink
pour for
pourquoi why
pouvoir can, to be able
pratiquant(e) (m, f) a believer who
  attends church regularly
précipiter (se) to hurry

préférer to prefer
premier(-ière) first
prendre to take; to drink
préoccuper(se) to be worried
près near
presque almost
pressé(e) in a hurry
prier to beg, to ask
principal(e) principal
principe (m) principle
prix (m) price
prochain(e) next
produit (m) product
professeur (m, f) teacher
profond(e) profound
propre clean
publicité (f) advertisements, publicity
publier to publish
puis then

Q

quai (m) quay, dock
quand when
  quand même even so
quartier (m) neighborhood
quatre four
que that; what
quel(le)(s) which
quelque some
  quelque chose something
  quelques-uns some of them
queue (f) line
qui who
quinzaine (f) about fifteen
quitter to leave

R

raconter to relate
raison (f) right
  avoir raison to be right
raisonable reasonable
ralentir to slow down
rarement rarely
réalité (f) reality
  en réalité actually
reconnaissant(e) grateful
reconnaître to recognize
regarder to look at

règlement (m) regulation
regretter to regret
remarquer to notice
rencontre (f) meeting
remettre to recover
rentrer to return
réparer to repare
repas (m) meal
réserver to reserve
respirer to breathe
resquiller to cut in line
retourner to return
réunir (se) to meet
réussir to succeed
réveillon (m) celebration the night
  before Christmas
revoir to see again
  au revoir good-bye, see you later
révue (f) magazine
rien (ne) nothing
rier to laugh
rouler to travel
route (f) road, highway
rue (f) street

S

Sacré Coeur Sacred Heart
saint (m) saint
sale dirty
saleté (f) dirtiness
sans without
sauce (f) sauce
savoir to know
savoureux(-euse) savory
séance (f) presentation
secondaire secondary
selon according to
semaine (f) week
sembler to seem
sentiment (m) sentiment, feeling
sérieux(-ieuse) serious
service (m) service
servir to serve
seul(e) only
seulement only
sévèrement severely
si if
soeur (f) sister
soir (m) evening
sonner to honk; to ring
sorte (f) sort, kind

sortie going out, exit
sortir to go out
souci (m) worry
soudainement suddenly
souvenir (se) to remember
souvent often
sportif(-ive) sport
subitement suddenly
sud (m) south
suer to sweat
suivre to follow
supermarché (m) supermarket
supporter to stand
sûr sure
  bien sûr certainly
surveillant (m) overseer
sympathique nice

T

ta your
tabac (m) tobacco
tâcher to try
taire to quiet
  se taire to become quiet
te (t') you (to you)
tellement so
temps (m) time
tenir to take
terrasse (f) pavement in front of
  a café
tête (f) head
têtu(e) stubborn
théâtre theater
thème theme, subject
tiens! Well!
timide timid
toi you
ton your
tôt early
toucher to touch
toujours still; always
Touraine (f) province in Central France
  whose capital is Tours
tourner to turn
tout (tous) all
  tout de même even so
  tout le monde everyone
  tous les jours every day
travail (m) work
travailler to work

T continued

travailleur(-euse)   hard-working
traverser   to cross
très   very
tromper (se)   to make a mistake
trop   too much
trouver   to find
type *(slang)* **(m)**   guy

U

un(e)   a, an; one
usine (f)   factory

V

vacances (f pl)   vacation
valeur (f)   value
valoir   to be worth
   il vaut mieux   it would be better
veille (f)   the night before
venir   to come
vers   toward
verser   to spill, to pour
veston (m)   sport coat
viande (f)   meat
vie (f)   life
vieux (vieille)   old
ville (f)   city
vin (m)   wine
vitrine (f)   store window
voici   here is, are
voilà   there is, are
voir   to see
voiture (f)   automobile
voleur (m)   robber
votre   your
vouloir   to want to
vrai(e)   true
vraiment   truly

W

wagon (m)   car (of train)

Y

y   there

NTC INTERMEDIATE FRENCH-LANGUAGE MATERIALS

Computer Software
French Basic Vocabulary Builder
  on Computer

**Videocassette, Activity Book,
  and Instructor's Manual**
VidéoPasseport—Français

Conversation Books
Conversational French
A vous de parler
Au courant
Tour du monde francophone Series
  Visages du Québec
  Images d'Haïti
  Promenade dans Paris
  Zigzags en France
Getting Started in French
Parlons français

Puzzle and Word Game Books
Easy French Crossword Puzzles
Easy French Word Games
Easy French Grammar Puzzles
Easy French Vocabulary Games
Easy French Culture Puzzles
Easy French Word Games and Puzzles

**Text/Audiocassette Learning
  Packages**
Just Listen 'n Learn French
Just Listen 'n Learn French Plus
Conversational French in 7 Days
Sans Frontières
Practice & Improve Your French
Practice & Improve Your French Plus
How to Pronounce French Correctly

Intermediate Workbooks
Ecrivons mieux!
French Verb Drills

Black-Line and Duplicating Masters
The French Newspaper
The Magazine in French
French Verbs and Vocabulary Bingo
  Games
French Grammar Puzzles
French Culture Puzzles
French Word Games for Beginners
French Crossword Puzzles
French Word Games

Transparencies
Everyday Situations in French

Reference Books
French Verbs and Essentials of Grammar
Nice 'n Easy French Grammar
Guide to French Idioms
Guide to Correspondence in French

Bilingual Dictionaries
NTC's New College French and
  English Dictionary
NTC's Dictionary of *Faux Amis*

For further information or a current catalog, write:
National Textbook Company
a division of *NTC Publishing Group*
4255 West Touhy Avenue
Lincolnwood, Illinois 60646-1975 U.S.A.